THE PERILS
CONSOLIDATION

A discussion of Australian housing and urban development policies

Patrick N Troy

The Federation Press
1996

Acknowledgment

If the urban policies of the Commonwealth were not so ill informed and presented in such a disingenuous way there would not be a need for this contribution to the debate on Australia's cities. In that sense I must fully acknowledge the authors of government urban policies for the opportunity to write this book.

It has not been easy to find or verify the information or data used to justify policies designed to change Australian Cities. The task was made bearable by the good natured commitment of my colleague Rita Coles without whose energy and attention to detail this work could not have been completed.

I wish also to thank Max Neutze, Tim Bonyhady, Clem Lloyd, Henry Wardlaw and Dick Smyth who provided critical comments on an early draft of the manuscript and Don Audet, Hunter Water Corporation and Alex Yarovy, BHP who kindly provided valuable information on water use in steel manufacture.

Any errors of fact or misinterpretation are all my own work.

Published in Sydney by :
The Federaton Press
PO Box 45, Annandale, NSW, 2038
3/56-72 John St, Leichhardt, NSW, 2040
Ph (02) 552 2200. Fax (02) 552 1681

National Library of Australia
Cataloguing-in-Publication entry

Troy, Patrick N. (Patrick Nicol).
The perils of urban consolidation: a discussion of Australian housing and urban development policies.

Bibliography
Includes index.
ISBN 1 86287 211 2
1. Urban renewal - Australia. 2. City planning - Australia.
3. Housing policy - Australia. I. Title.
307.34160994

Typeset by The Urban Research Program, Research School of Social Sciences, Australian National University, Canberra ACT, 0200

Printed by Southwood Press Pty Ltd, Marrickville, NSW

Contents

Abbreviations

AGPS	Australian Government Publishing Service
AIHDC	Australian Housing Industry Development Council
ALP	Australian Labor Party
AMCORD	Australian Model Code for Residential Development
AURDR	Australian Urban and Regional Development Review
BBC	Building Better Cities
BTCE	Bureau of Transport & Communication Economics
CCC	Cumberland City Council
CT	Canberra Times
DHHCS	Department of Health, Housing & Community Services
DITAC	Department of Industry Technology & Commerce
EPAA	*Environmental Planning and Assessment Act* 1979 (NSW)
HALCS	Housing and Locational Choice Survey
HARD	Department of Housing & Regional Development
HIA	Housing Industry Association
IC	Industry Commission
LEP	Local Environment Plan
MFP	Multi Function Polis
NHS	National Housing Strategy
SEPP	State Environmental Planning Policy
SREP	State Regional Environment Plan

The Australian National University

With Compliments

Patrick N. Troy AO

Professor and Head

Urban Research Program

Research School of Social Sciences

Canberra ACT 0200
FAX No (06) 249-0312

Telephone: (06) 249-2297
Internet : patrick.troy@anu.edu.au

All you have to do now is get all the public
libraries in your area to order it.
Tell your friends to buy it.
Get on to your local GP to prescribe it as the
only non-addictive sleeping cure that has no
known dangerous side effects

List of Tables

THE PERILS OF URBAN CONSOLIDATION

INTRODUCTION

From the earliest days of settlement governments have pursued policies which affect the form and structure of Australian cities. But in no period have the Commonwealth Government and State governments displayed as much energy or determination to change our cities as they have done over the recent past. They have defied expressions of individual and social desire, acted King Canute-like to deny the tide of economic forces. State governments have bullied and emasculated local government in pursuit of their objectives. In taking this path, Commonwealth and State governments have ignored unpalatable evidence and taken advice only from those they know agree with their position. They have attempted to stifle debate and to direct research consultancies to reward supporters.

Proponents of the present policies justify their actions on the grounds of the fashionable need to respond to *globalisation*. The measures employed, however, may more properly be seen as an attempt to reduce housing and development standards.

The present suite of urban policies have created a situation in which to be conservative is to be radical. That is, a conservative defence of traditional forms of urban development in Australian cities is a radical defence of housing standards and residential amenity.

The argument presented in this book is that infrastructure costs and environmental stresses can and should be reduced. But it points out that these objectives can be achieved without changing the traditional form of our cities. Indeed the argument is that the traditional form of our cites may give us our best chance of reducing environmental stress.

Chapter 1

FLAWS IN THE FIGURES OR DEMOGRAPHIC CHANGES AND HOUSING CHOICE

The earliest efforts to regulate housing in Australia grew out of a concern for safety and health—in particular the need to reduce overcrowding (Troy 1988, 1992). The parks and gardens movement of the early twentieth century and the earliest efforts to introduce town planning were also directed to improve health, amenity, environmental quality, equity and efficiency in the city (Sandercock 1975). The garden city movement and its impact on the Australian city is one example of the pursuit of notions of equity and the desire for a more healthy urban environment (Freestone 1989).

In the early post-World War II period in Australia the uncoordinated and *leap frogging* of development which resulted in pockets of urban development in which housing was separated from shopping, community facilities (where provided at all) and employment and interspersed with rural uses and vacant land withdrawn from productive use—and called *sprawl*—made it extremely difficult to efficiently provide urban services. The progressive introduction of town planning and development control measures during that period made it easier for servicing and local government authorities to meet the demand for services which arose from increasing expectations and the rapid growth of the urban population. The benefits of town planning and development control measures are now obvious in the more equitable and efficient provision of services and in the elimination of wasteful *sprawl*.

The determination in the early post-World War II period to ensure that the population was adequately housed and that slums were eliminated led to the establishment of minimum housing standards. There was general recognition that the private sector could not be relied on to provide sufficient housing of adequate standard for low income households and agreement that there was a need for public intervention in the supply of housing to meet the demand. Commonwealth Government policies in the early 1950s aimed at raising the level of owner occupation while increasing the supply of housing for low income households. The use of housing production to stimulate the economy had the effect of increasing the supply while the emphasis on owner occupation ensured that housing was provided in an egalitarian way. The net effect was that housing was both relatively equally provided in terms of quality and its ownership was more equitably spread through the society.

Recent housing policy initiatives have been developed with little understanding of the origins of government involvement in housing. Beginning in 1978 the Commonwealth has sought to withdraw from the provision of public housing. The insistence by the Commonwealth of the introduction of market related rents in 1978 together with its continuing insistence on targeting public housing to low income groups has resulted in the gradual conversion of the State public housing authorities to authorities delivering residual or welfare housing. The Australian Labor Party's (ALP) 1982 promise that, in government, the Commonwealth would double the proportion of housing in the public sector within a decade (ALP 1982: 175), that is, by raising the proportion of public housing from 5 to 10 per cent within ten years, has fallen well short of the target. At the 1981 census 4.9 per cent of housing was owned by housing authorities and a further 1.4 per cent was owned by other government agencies. By 1991 these figures were 5.6 and 1.2 per cent respectively. In addition, by 1994 the overwhelming majority of tenants in State housing authority dwellings had their rents subsidised and a substantial proportion were tenants in receipt of a welfare benefit.

Simultaneously, recent government urban policy has been developed with seemingly little understanding of the origins of urban planning or why Australian cities take their present form or structure.

This book has two purposes: to discuss the origins of recent housing and urban policies and to explore some of the misinterpretations, myths, fallacies and paradoxes which have served as justifications for them; and to suggest an alternative approach to the development of policy in these areas which takes fuller account of the environmental and infrastructural issues as well as the basic demand for accommodation. This alternative approach to housing and urban policy is based on a more complete, less partial consideration of social, environmental and economic processes than that embodied in the current policy initiatives. The book concentrates on the situation in the State capitals, particularly Sydney and Melbourne but also uses evidence from Canberra.

I Origin of the Present Policy Dilemmas

The present function, form and structure of Australia's major cities are essentially the product of nineteenth century economic and political processes. With the exception of Canberra the political and administrative centres are the same today as they were then. Some market centres have waxed and waned in importance but those which served as regional centres in the nineteenth century retain their significance today. Some towns have become more important as industrial centres. Others have declined and even disappeared, especially some of those built on mining. We now have fun towns like the Gold Coast. But, by and large, Australian cities essentially discharge the same *set* of functions in government, education, cultural activities, health services, commerce and manufacturing today as they did in the nineteenth century.

The economic and political processes which have occurred, however, have resulted in the evolution of extensive cities with highly centralised political and economic power and highly centralised transport systems. But as they have grown and become more extensive, commerce, employment and recreational activities have become more decentralised. The centralised structure of each of the cities was initially determined by the location of colonial power and commerce. In the port cities like Sydney and Melbourne the initial colonial administration, commerce, warehousing and industrial development occurred close to the harbour. Subsequent incremental growth reinforced the importance of the initial development. As the State and city road system grew it focused on the centre, and later the development of the public transport system—first the tram then the train—further strengthened the centralisation.

The form of early development was determined by the importance of domestic production (Mullins 1981a, 1981b), the need to cope with wastes on site and preference for the detached single family residence. The early towns were essentially suburban in form although both Sydney and Melbourne experienced a wave of consolidation through the construction of terrace housing, much of it jerry-built rental housing, in the late nineteenth century. (It is apposite to note here that many of the building regulations currently in force in those cities contain hangovers from attempts to curb the worst abuses perpetrated by some of the developers of that period.) The development of railways and tramways facilitated the growth of the towns into highly centralised cities in which single family detached housing was even more the dominant form of accommodation. Later still, widespread car ownership allowed the suburbs to spread further but did not challenge the primacy of the city centre. Sydney experienced another period of consolidation in the late 1920s and 1930s when flats proliferated, especially in its eastern suburbs. That period of consolidation was brought to an end by the war and by widespread opposition to flat construction on a variety of grounds including the poor quality accommodation and environment which resulted.

Over the post-World War II period a series of social changes have been attended by technological changes. Developments in retailing, marine and air transport, information technology and office organisation have reduced the emphasis on the central business district (CBD). Innovations in materials handling, hydraulic systems and the development of small electric motors have radically changed the organisation and location of warehouses and factories. Simultaneously innovations occurred in structural and materials engineering. The cumulative effect of these changes led to Sydney and Melbourne developing multiple centres most of which are quite small. Brisbane, Adelaide and Perth have experienced similar changes, although on a smaller scale.

Although there have been major changes in the scale, nature and relationships between activities carried out in the cities, the political institutional framework within which these changes have occurred has been little changed. The postwar development of urban planning did not disturb the hierarchy of power within the State administrations which remains much as it was a hundred years ago. All States (save Queensland), however, have now replaced statutory planning authorities by central government ministries. Local government remains the creature of the State government but is now more tightly controlled. Its functions and boundaries, however appropriate at the time of their individual incorporation, are frequently inappropriate as a foundation for coping with the problems presented by the development and operation of the modern city.

For the most part the infrastructure services provided in the cities use nineteenth century technologies, are delivered according to nineteenth century notions of quality, service delivery and access and are financed by highly centralised, hierarchic organisations. Many of these services were delivered by statutory authorities which were created with a high degree of independence to avoid detailed involvement of politicians in their operations to reduce nepotism, cronyism and to ensure they operated efficiently. This independence has always been problematic; State governments have never been able to fully accept the need for them to operate in accordance with prudent business principles. The pressures on them from governments to keep tariffs low for short term political reasons gradually eroded their independence and their capacity to finance their expansion and even their operation. Politicians have always sought to use them to dispense patronage to favour development in one area over another and so on. The result is that, as the major cities grew rapidly in the post-World War II period by a process of peripheral incremental expansion, the authorities have not been able to meet the demand for their services. This is most evident in the water supply, sewerage and drainage services but also partially explains why there was little development of public transport. The recent pursuit of managerialist policies has resulted in the remolding of some of the powerful service authorities—which are increasingly being corporatised and privatised—with consequential loss of the democratic control, which statutory authorities and government departments both afford.

The Commonwealth assumed responsibility for income taxes to help prosecute the war effort during World War II, and over the postwar period gradually increased its financial power over the States and, through them, over local government. Politics at the Commonwealth level is often presented as a contest between two main groups with different attitudes to the distribution of wealth in the community and to the desirability of intervention by government in the operation of the economy but it may also be characterised in part as a competition between the political parties to reduce taxes. The result is that Commonwealth governments have increasingly had limited resources to invest in infrastructure services and have sought to withdraw from funding housing programs. The reduction of income from the Commonwealth led to a fiscal crisis in the States. State and local governments responded by introducing imposts on developers as a way of meeting the demand for services.

One response has been for governments to try to shift more of the responsibility for provision of services to developers. Initially governments sought contributions from developers for reticulation of water supply and sewerage and the provision of local roads and drains. Local councils began to require developers to provide for roads, footpaths and drainage in the 1950s. Developer charges were introduced in Sydney in 1961 by the Water Board and quickly followed in other cities. Later the imposts were increased to include a wider range of local services and facilities and contributions were required towards *headworks* costs where this was a relevant consideration. One of the beneficial effects of this policy of requiring developer contributions was that it helped the planners achieve their objectives of reducing scattered development of the major cities and ensured that adequate provision was made for services such as open space, community facilities and landscaping. But the developer contributions had four aspects which were less advantageous. The first was that their imposition did not result in appropriate economic signals being given to the providers of the services because they focused attention on the capital costs of the reticulation system but not the recurrent costs of the system as a whole; secondly they cut off the appropriate feedback information from the service authorities to the planners for the development of the city's structure; thirdly they led to significant inequity between the owners of already serviced property which had had services funded from the general revenue of the service agencies or local government and later buyers of property; and finally inequity between existing owners and those who came later, whether as children of the existing population or as migrants. A fuller discussion of these issues may be found in Neutze (1994).

This seemingly open ended extraction of finance for urban services from the developers reached a point in the early 1980s where the costs of service provision were a large proportion of the costs of an urban block. In spite of these imposts, State governments still faced increasing demands for capital for the wide variety of urban services.

Rather than rethink the way urban services were priced or provided in order to meet the demand for them, State governments sought alternative ways of moderating demand. The solution most favoured was to pursue a policy of consolidation, also called *urban containment* or the development of *compact cities*. Under this policy it was thought that consolidation would reduce the demand on governments for infrastructure capital in several ways:

- by increasing density in the inner areas, where it was argued there was excess capacity in the full range of services, governments hoped to defer construction of additional infrastructure;
- as a result of reducing the size of new housing allotments and increasing the proportion of medium and high density dwellings in new development governments expected that the length of pipes, wires and roads, needed to service the new areas of expansion would be reduced;
- by increasing density governments expected more people to use public transport (especially fixed rail modes); and
- with a more compact city personal and freight delivery trips would be shorter.

By the mid 1980s the declining population and especially the fall in school enrolments in the inner areas began to cause concern. Governments were facing a situation where new fringe developments needed schools yet there appeared to be surplus capacity in the existing areas. The situation was compounded by the fact that declining family sizes meant that a given area of development produced lower school enrolments than had occurred only a generation earlier when the planning system based on primary school catchment areas had been developed. Changing views about educational quality and choice and therefore increasing the optimum size of secondary schools meant that fewer secondary schools were needed. The additional effect was that opening new secondary schools in new areas led to greater pressure to close schools in existing areas.

There was also a view among Labor State governments and councils that increasing the population in the inner areas would help preserve the political geography of the city by ensuring that there were sufficient low income residents to *out vote* the owners of commercial property in inner city council elections or the new, higher income residents which resulted from gentrification of the inner areas and, thus, the continuation of Labor representation for State government electorates which covered the inner city areas. Liberal governments, however, frequently intervened in central city administration to protect or advance central city business interests while favouring consolidation. Consolidation policies were first introduced in Sydney in the early 1980s and justified on the grounds of the alleged savings in infrastructure which would be reflected in savings in public capital requirements.

The policy was resisted by local governments throughout Sydney which found themselves facing laws and regulations introduced by the New South Wales State Government seriously reducing their capacity to control local development. In the face of spirited opposition, State governments developed an environmental argument to rationalise their policies: they sought to justify their position by arguing that environmental benefits would flow from the consolidation policy, adding to the benefits it was claimed would result from more efficient provision and use of infrastructure. Similar processes and arguments followed in other States and Territories.

Consolidation was also favoured by some environmentalists on the grounds that higher density living would be accompanied by a reduction in greenhouse gases due to shorter journeys, reduced use of the motor car and increased travel by public transport. It was also thought that increased density would reduce *sprawl*—a word adopted from American debates and which had no objective meaning in Australian description of contemporary urban areas. In America *sprawl* meant inefficient, uncoordinated, development—the same as it had in Australia in the early postwar period. Although this was no longer the situation in Australian cities the emotive and pejorative content in the word made it attractive to contemporary Australian commentators who used it to denote *extensive development*. It was argued that reducing sprawl or extensive development would lead to more compact cities which in turn would reduce investment in infrastructure, increase public transport usage and reduce the conversion of agricultural and bush lands to urban development.

In all States governments and their advisers also advanced quasi-demographic arguments. They drew attention to the changes in household size and the ageing of the population which had occurred over the previous 20 years and argued that traditional suburban expansion of houses on separate allotments did not meet the rapidly growing needs of the smaller households. It was also claimed that consolidation policies would result in cheaper housing and greater choice.

The arguments have a superficial attraction and simple elegance which appeals to those swayed by *common sense* but they rely on a flawed interpretation of the data and a misunderstanding of the social processes that are occurring.

II Commonwealth Involvement in Urban Policy

The Commonwealth has a clear interest in housing and urban issues. Its constitutional responsibilities in these fields are limited but it nonetheless has progressively, if at an uneven rate, developed policies and taken initiatives in a number of areas at different periods (Troy & Lloyd 1981). The Whitlam Governments of 1972–1975 attempted to influence the distribution of the population by developing a regional development policy. They sought to create more equitable cities by developing more equal access to urban services including the completion of the sewerage systems. Whitlam endeavoured to increase efficiency of urban Australia by a better planned development process including more active intervention in the land development process and to reduce the rate of inflation in urban land prices. His governments sought to develop better public transport, give greater commitment to public housing and create the conditions for a more informed debate and better urban administration by insisting that the information bases be improved. Whitlam encouraged more independence and democratic involvement of local government including increasing its financial independence. His governments increased protection of the environment and preserved significant elements of the National Estate. Most importantly, this was all done with the cooperation and active engagement of the States—not always with the same degree of enthusiasm or with the same degree of progress in each policy area at the same time. Because his governments focussed on programs designed to change the process of decision making rather than attempt to deliver some product they achieved a high degree of success.

While the Fraser Governments of 1975–1983 withdrew from many of the areas and lacked the larger vision to which the Whitlam Governments had worked, they continued with Commonwealth engagement in housing policy, local government financial support, improved urban data bases and various infrastructure issues.

The 1982 ALP Platform (ALP 1982) promised that a Labor Government would take an active role in urban policy fields including establishing a Department of Urban and Regional Affairs. The Hawke Labor Government elected in 1983 failed to honour these commitments. The first Hawke Ministry did not acknowledge that Australian urban areas faced a series of problems which were steadily worsening. There was a convenient and persistently repeated misperception in that Ministry that the Whitlam Governments had fallen because of their engagement with urban issues. Nowhere in the Hawke Governments was there any vision of the urban nature of Australia or how the system of cities needed to be made more equitable and efficient. The Accords under which the union movement agreed to forgo or moderate wage claims in return for commitments to improving the *social wage* (meaning increased investment by the Commonwealth in urban services) were successively breached (Stilwell 1986).

By 1987 the Commonwealth had withdrawn so far from any coherent set of policies on urban issues it dismantled the housing portfolio, allocating elements of responsibility for housing to a number of Departments which pursued conflicting objectives. This meant that a number of Ministers had responsibility for an *ad hoc* set of aspects of housing and urban policy. This was the climate in which that embarrassing farce of the so-called Multi Function Polis (MFP) was conceived. This project emerged from an initiative by Japanese politicians and officials to build a modern city. It was to be a large-scale experiment in creating the *city of the future.* The Australian response was made by a Minister not known for his expertise on urban issues, who was supported by a Department in which there was no knowledge at the senior levels of the Australian urban system—even less of the Japanese urban system or its problems—and little appreciation of the history of urban Utopian proposals throughout the world. It was believed that the MFP would be an experiment to show how the private sectors of two countries could successfully marshal the resources, human and financial, to create a new urban lifestyle and environment. The most charitable assessments of the proposal acknowledge that it was *an idea before its time.* More sceptical critics believe the process involved in the site selection was seriously flawed and that the exercise was a waste of scarce resources. The proposed project nonetheless had the effect of diverting attention from the problems clearly emerging in the cities as they became more polarised and were suffering stresses due to continued cutbacks in the level of infrastructure investment.

Following the collapse of the economy in 1988 which placed the States under even greater pressure, the Commonwealth began hesitantly to re-engage with some urban issues. The Minister for Housing and Aged Care commissioned a National Housing Policy Review in 1989 which undertook a narrowly conceived review of the Commonwealth State Housing Agreement. The Review's report to the Department of Community Services and Health was inadequately researched and was barely acknowledged. This was followed in 1990 by another review whose terms of reference were more widely drawn. The National Housing Strategy (NHS) was an internal review carried out within the bureaucracy by people who had no established reputation either as housing researchers or administrators of housing programs. Although it sponsored a number of *background papers,* including some prepared by people outside the bureaucracy, the NHS was always under the control of the Minister for Health, Housing and Community Development which seriously limited its opportunities for a rigorous, independent, research-based review of housing and urban development policies in Australia. Much of its report was directed to producing an argument to support policy positions which had already been adopted. It gave special weight to the arguments favouring consolidation.

Following the 1993 election housing and regional development responsibilities at the Commonwealth level were brought together in the Department of Housing and Regional Development (HARD). Commonwealth recognition of the significance of housing and urban and regional issues appeared at last to be confirmed. However, the Commonwealth then announced three initiatives which indicated lack of agreement of purpose or understanding of the issues: a Review of Regional Development announced in July 1993 by Alan Griffiths, Minister for Industry Technology and Regional Development, under the Chairmanship of Mr Bill Kelty whose report *Developing Australia: A Regional Perspective* (the Kelty Report) was submitted in December 1993; the Australian Urban and Regional Development Review announced in 1993 by Brian Howe, Minister for Housing and Regional Development under the Chairpersonship of Ms Jenny Macklin and the Prime Minister's Urban DesignTask Force convened by Mr John Mant whose report *Urban Design in Australia* (the Mant Report) was published in November 1994. (The first led by someone with no previously known expertise on regional issues, the second by someone with no acknowledged expertise in either housing or urban affairs and the third led by a Sydney lawyer.) In this period the Commonwealth Government also gave a number of references to the Industries Commission on public housing (1993), urban transport (1994), and financing of infrastructure (1991). The multiplicity of Reviews and Industries Commission references served only to indicate confusion and lack of purpose at the Commonwealth level.

Instead of taking advantage of its distance from the pressing problems of the moment and first exploring the issues or developing expertise in the area, the Commonwealth chose to articulate the arguments in favour of consolidation which had been rehearsed by the States. The Commonwealth had responsibility for one urban area, Canberra, and it was also playing a leading role in developing national building codes but it had been trying to scale down its involvement in housing policy issues for some time.

The Commonwealth's promulgation of the suite of policies it adopted in favour of consolidation was in part a means of resolving the tensions and inconsistencies of its own position and of responding to the pressures placed on it by the States for resources to help them meet the emerging problems of their cities.

In summary, current Commonwealth housing and urban policy has not grown out of any continuous evolution of understanding or commitment, though the Commonwealth nonetheless has clear interests and responsibilities in the area. The arguments the Commonwealth has employed to justify its current urban policy have three roots: demographic changes, infrastructure considerations and environmental impacts, which we will now explore in turn. Because the book attempts to explore these separately and they are inevitably related there is necessarily a degree of repetition. This will be most apparent in Chapter 3 where the case for each of the different but related areas of environmental concern is relatively self-contained.

The demographic arguments for consolidation are that household size is falling, house size is increasing, the population is ageing and needs more smaller dwellings. From this it is concluded that we should try to obtain a more *efficient* fit between the distribution of household size and the distribution of dwelling size by increasing density. The argument for increasing density also claims that to do so would provide better choice of housing and lifestyles. This chapter will explore these arguments.

The average size of households has fallen over the postwar period and, by definition, the occupancy rate of dwellings has fallen. Some politicians have concluded from this that dwellings are too large and we should adopt policies designed to force a change in the distribution of dwelling sizes. This, it is claimed, will lead to a stock of housing which is much closer to the emerging demand. It is interesting to note here that the green belt fracas of the late 1950s in Sydney had their origin in a refusal by the Cumberland County Council (CCC) to acknowledge the rapid postwar decline in household size in the established suburbs. By regarding the residential capacity of these suburbs as fixed at the 1946 level and counting people rather than households the CCC greatly underestimated the demand for new residential land on the fringe. The current policy initiatives may be seen as simple replays of the same misguided policies of the late 1950s and early 1960s and may have the same sad impact on the quality of urban development.

The data referred to are usually aggregate national cross sectional data collected at the various censuses conducted since 1947 and set out in Table 1.1.

A major problem with the data is that, like many comparisons, the rate of decline in household size depends on the period of analysis. The beginning of the period was one when there was a massive shortage of housing following the Depression and World War II when little housing was built. This resulted in overcrowding and an excessive occupancy rate. Housing shortages existed through the 1950s. We might even argue that it was not until 1961 or later that the housing shortage was overcome (Greig 1995a, 1995b). After the war living standards rose and people demanded more comfortable, commodious accommodation. It would seem inappropriate then, to conclude that because the occupancy rate has fallen we now have an oversupply of accommodation or that dwellings are in some way too large. There is no evidence of an unmet demand for smaller dwellings.

Table 1.1

Average Household Size and Persons per Dwelling 1947 to 1986 Census

Year	Persons per Household	Persons per Dwelling
1947	3.8	3.9
1954	3.6	3.6
1961	3.6	3.5
1966	3.5	3.4
1971	3.3	3.2
1976	3.1	2.9
1981	3.0	2.8
1986	2.9	2.7

Source: Persons per Household 1947–1954 – Australia Year Books; Persons per Household 1961–1986 – Indicative Planning Council for the Housing Industry, Long Term Projections Report 1989, Table A5; Persons per Dwelling – *Housing Australia: A Statistical Overview* Cat No 1320.0, 1992, Table 2.6.

Note: As enumerated on census night, no adjustment made for household members temporarily absent. Before the 1986 Census, caravans in caravan parks were treated as non-private dwellings.

A technical point about these data is that there were substantial changes in the census definitions of both *private dwellings* and *dwellings* during the period. The census defined a dwelling as the space occupied by one household. This approximation may be close enough for some purposes at the national level but in certain areas, especially in the cities which are the focus of the housing policy concern, the approximation is misleading because of the higher likelihood of the fall in multiple occupancy in those areas, which would tend to exaggerate the decline in household size.

The rural population fell from 30 per cent in 1947 to 15 per cent in 1986 although the absolute numbers fell very little. The *rural* population changed from one related to farming to one more engaged in ex-urban living, holiday, recreation activities and retirement, especially in coastal regions. The decline in the population related to farming led to a decline in rural dwelling occupancy. Ex-urban, holiday, recreational and retirement housing tends to have lower occupancy rates. Including this housing as part of the functional urban housing stock tends to show lower occupancy rates than has been experienced in urban areas. The decline in household size has been used to justify a change in urban housing policy. To include urban with non-urban areas and to compare the average size of occupied private dwellings with households over the period is like comparing apples with oranges. One consequence of this elision in definition of the unit of analysis and the inclusion of urban with non-urban housing is that it tends to exaggerate the *decline in household size* over the period. This means it is essential to separately analyse the housing situation in rural Australia compared with the situation in the urban areas.

It is apposite to note here that over the past 20 years Federal Governments have followed a variety of policies designed to encourage the development of retirement villages and homes for the aged. The move by the aged to retirement villages tends to exaggerate the decline in household size because formerly many of these individuals lived during their declining years with their relatives. That is, the move from the extended family home to retirement villages will tend to reduce household size in the later period. On the other hand the recent tendency for the aged to move into hostel, nursing home or retirement village accommodation will have tended to reduce the size of households and simultaneously reduce the number of one and two person households, but the net effect of this process is yet unclear (hostels and nursing homes are classified as *non-private* so those moving into them are not included in the household size statistics).

III Proportion of Households with One or Two Members

The fact that the various Australian censuses (Table 1.2) show that the proportion of one or two person households has increased has excited much interest. Much of this increase is a natural consequence of the fall in family size, older age at marriage, increasing freedom and economic independence of women and general increase in living standards. The almost complete disappearance of boarding houses from the inner city areas has meant that many one person households which formerly would not have been counted in the statistics because they would have been classified as living in *non-private* accommodation now occupy flats or houses. Apart from the obvious point that the change from the average size of occupied private dwelling to average size of household has tended to exaggerate the decrease because dwellings previously containing several households are now separately counted we can agree that the proportion of one and two person households has indeed increased. But what is the significance of this fact?

It is argued, from an *efficiency* point of view, that this has resulted in many households living in dwellings "too large" for them. From this it is implied that many would prefer to shift to smaller houses/dwellings if they were available or indeed, that they *should*. While there has been little evidence of this preference among older households Commonwealth Ministers have nonetheless persisted with the view that older households should move. There seems to be no reason why smaller households should not have some spare capacity in their dwellings if they feel they need it and can continue to afford it.

The censuses reveal that a significant proportion of one and two person households already live in smaller dwellings and have done since 1947. About half the one and two person households in Australia in 1986 lived in smaller housing (that is, in dwellings with one or two bedrooms) (Table 1. 3). Although the proportion has fallen we note that for the Sydney Statistical Division the proportion of one and two person households living in one and two bedroom dwellings is almost 60 per cent and in the Melbourne Statistical Division nearly 54 per cent. This raises the question: what proportion of the smaller households living in smaller dwellings would be regarded as acceptable? There is no evidence that the demand for that form of housing is not being met by the market.

Table 1.2

Household Size Distribution: Australia 1947 to 1986

Persons in Household[a]	1947	1954	1961	1966	1971	1976	1981	1986
				per cent of total households				
1	8.1	9.0	10.3	11.8	13.6	15.7	18.0	19.5
2	20.3	23.2	23.7	24.7	26.5	28.1	29.1	30.0
Total 1 & 2	**28.4**	**32.2**	**34.0**	**36.5**	**40.1**	**43.8**	**47.1**	**49.5**
3	21.6	21.1	19.1	18.4	18.0	17.3	16.9	17.1
4	20.5	20.5	19.9	19.1	18.7	19.4	19.1	18.6
5	13.6	13.1	13.5	13.0	12.2	11.2	10.5	9.6
6	7.7	6.9	7.3	7.1	6.3	5.0	4.1	3.5
7	4.1	3.2	3.4	2.7	2.7	1.3	0.9	1.1
8+	4.1	2.7	2.8	2.7	2.1	1.3	0.9	0.7

Source: 1954, 1966, 1976, 1981, 1986 – Indicative Planning Council for the Housing Industry, Long Term Projections Report, 1989, Table A8; 1947, 1955, 1961 and 1966 Australia Year Books; 1971 Commonwealth Census of Australia Bulletin 2.

Note: (a) As enumerated on census night, no adjustment made for members temporarily absent. Before the 1986 Census, caravans in caravan parks were treated as non-private dwellings.

Table 1.3

Proportion of 'Smaller' Households Living in 'Smaller' Accommodation: Australia, Sydney, Melbourne, Remainder of State or State Total

Year		Total 1 &2 Person Households	One and Two Person Households Living in Dwellings of : 1 Bedroom[a] N	1 Bedroom[a] %	2 Bedrooms N	2 Bedrooms %	Total N	Total %
1971	Australia	1,470,282	225,189	19.7	572,032	38.9	797,221	54.2
	Sydney SD	356,431	63,962	24.1	157,326	44.1	221,228	62.1
	Rem NSW	204,981	27,095	16.5	80,810	39.4	107,905	52.6
	Melb SD	288,674	52,262	22.8	118,773	41.1	171,035	59.3
	Rem VIC	107,794	9568	11.3	34,487	32.0	44,055	40.9
1976[b]	Australia	1,796,853	249,591	13.9	665,423	37.0	915,014	50.9
	NSW Total	665,968	101,778	15.3	278,662	41.8	380,440	57.1
	VIC Total	480,710	68,400	14.2	178,988	37.2	247,388	51.5
1981[c]	Australia	2,200,831	302,868	13.8	903,454	41.1	1,206,322	54.8
1986	Australia	2,566,600	277,316	10.8	1,013,705	39.5	1,291,021	50.3
	Sydney SD	570,537	78,018	13.7	262,556	45.9	339,584	59.5
	Rem NSW	333,339	31,714	9.5	127,900	38.4	159,614	47.9
	Melb SD	466,193	55,634	11.9	194,772	41.8	250,406	53.7
	Rem VIC	191,643	15,097	7.9	62,437	32.6	77,534	40.5

Source: Australian Bureau of Statistics, Census of Population and Housing 1971 to 1986

Note: (a) One bedroom classification includes dwellings with no bedroom; (b) comparable data for Sydney and Melbourne not readily available; (c) comparable data for Sydney, New South Wales, Melbourne and Victoria not readily available

Table 1.4

Percentage of Occupied Private Dwellings by Number of Rooms: Australia

Year	1	2	3	4	5	6+	NS	Estimated Median Size Dwelling (Number of Rooms)
				per cent				
1947	3.1	4.3	7.2	22.2	30.9	31.8	0.5	4.2
1954	2.3	4.0	6.4	19.3	31.3	36.4	0.3	4.4
1961	1.4	3.1	5.6	17.4	34.4	37.7	0.4	4.5
1966	1.6	3.3	5.7	15.7	35.3	38.4	n.a.	4.7
1971	1.9	3.7	6.9	17.3	37.8	32.4	n.a.	4.6
1976	0.5	1.7	4.7	14.5	29.7	46.6	2.3	4.6
1981	0.6	1.4	4.6	15.3	28.1	48.4	1.6	5.0

Sources: Census of the Commonwealth of Australia 1947, Vol III, Detailed Tables, Parts XX–XXVIII, Statisticians Report, Australian Life Table, Table 5; Census of the Commonwealth of Australia 1961, Census Bulletin No 22, Summary of Dwellings for Australia, Table 4; Census of the Commonwealth of Australia 1971, Bulletin 2, Part 9, Table 3; Summary Characteristics of Persons and Dwellings, Australia, Cat No 2443.0, Table 36; ; *Housing Australia* 1992, Cat No 1320.0, Appendix, Table 3.3; Australia in Profile 1988, Cat No 2502.0: 60.

Note: In the 1986 Census, data on the number of rooms per dwelling were not recorded and subsequently not collected in the 1991 Census.

To summarise: the fall in average household size and the increase in the proportion of one and two person households is, in part, a function of the way the statistics are constructed; in part, the result of the aged person housing policies which have been pursued; in part the loss of boarding houses; in part, the reflection of falling family size; and the market outcomes of the people who have been able to afford their preferred housing because of rising living standards over the postwar period. The simultaneous apparent increase in dwelling size per person reflects these processes. Dwellings consist of a discrete number of rooms and although rooms may be added to houses to meet changing demand for accommodation, this is more difficult for other types of dwelling. Few are reduced in size. But there is great flexibility and choice in the way the conventional detached housing may be used, especially as the household size falls. Housing policy ought not seek to deny occupants the opportunity to take advantage of this flexibility.

IV Average Size of Dwelling

Another point laboured in the debates is that while the average household size has fallen, the average size of dwelling is said to have increased. But there is much confusion as to what the situation actually is. Much of the confusion arises because of the difference between a *house* and a *dwelling*. All houses are dwellings but not all dwellings are houses. Dwellings include flats, apartments, terrace houses, patio houses, town houses, semi-detached houses—indeed all the forms of private accommodation (other than caravans and other temporary forms of shelter) in which households live. The censuses (Table 1.4) suggest that there has been an increase in terms of the estimated median number of rooms in occupied private dwellings in the postwar period. The census figures suggest that, in terms of number of rooms, the size of dwellings remained stable from 1961 to 1976 and increased by about nine per cent between 1976 and 1981; much of this increase is thought to be due to alterations and additions to the stock of dwellings as households modernised their dwellings and made themselves more comfortable by adding *family rooms* and other living space. In terms of rooms designated as bedrooms the housing stock has been remarkably stable over the period 1971–1986 with approximately half all dwellings having three bedrooms and another quarter having two (*see Housing Australia* 1992: 37, table 3.1). It is clear from the figures that there was a substantial increase in the number of larger dwellings between 1971 and 1981. Numbers of rooms were not recorded in either 1986 or 1991.

But the reason for the excitement is the reported increase in the average size of *new houses* in Australia which are claimed to have increased from 130 to 187 square metres between 1970 and 1989 (note that the NHS (1991a, 1992a) misquoted the figures: the average floor area for new houses in 1989 was 196 square metres and that for 1990 was 187 square metres (Table 1.5)). There are several aspects of these ABS data which are ignored. The first is that the data indicate that the distribution of house sizes changed dramatically over the period although government spokesmen never give any indication of the distribution of house size. The increase in construction of very large houses was for a small proportion of the market yet it had a marked effect on the average. The distribution of new house sizes in Sydney and Melbourne for example appears to have been bi-modal through the 1980s (Figures 1 & 2, Appendix), with a small proportion of extremely large houses causing a dramatic increase in the average. This should have alerted the government's advisers to the danger of using simple averages without information on the distribution. (The distribution in the later period appears to be bi-modal because of the intervals chosen for presentation of the data—it is more likely that the real distribution is highly skewed whereas it does not appear to have been so heavily skewed at the beginning of the period.) If we exclude the houses over 250 square metres (which had an average size of 333 square metres in 1988–1989 and 336 square metres in 1989–1990 in Sydney; and 553 square metres in 1988–1989 and 340 square metres in 1989–1990 in Melbourne) the average size of new houses built in Sydney in 1989 was 156 square metres (Figure 3, Appendix) and in Melbourne in 1989 was 151 square metres which was the average for most of the decade (Figure 4 Appendix).

The data used to derive these averages are the returns made by local authorities on approvals for construction activity in their areas. These returns are notoriously incomplete and imprecise. The estimate of size is used to *check* figures to ensure that the estimate of value (on which individual building permit fees are based) is reasonable—little effort goes into checking whether the estimate of house size in the individual returns is itself accurate. The returns on building approvals from local authorities also frequently fail to include estimates on size. More critical is the fact that the data cited are for house approvals. The data on number of commencements are not consistently related to approvals and in any event commencement returns do not have estimates for size of house. There are no estimates for the size of houses actually built. There is a varying relationship between approvals and actual completions depending on the stage in the business cycle. The relationship between approved size of house and actual size built is likely to be most variable at the point at which the cycle peaks. It is most likely to overstate the size at that point. That is, the average size of house approvals for 1989, which was when the boom ended, is most likely to be larger than the average size of those completed. While the average size of new houses has probably increased it has not done so to the extent that politicians and some of their advisers have claimed.

Secondly, while on average *new houses* may have increased in size we cannot simply assert that the average size of the stock of *dwellings* has increased. The data relate to the flows of *new houses* not to the flow of *new dwellings* and the relation of the size of these new houses to the size of the stock of dwellings can only be guessed at. This is not a minor or irritating technical point. For example the flow data excludes consideration of flats which would significantly reduce the average size of new dwellings, and also of conversion of houses which would cause a fall in average size over time.

Over the period there were several processes occurring which would have resulted in an apparent increase in size of houses. The first was that this was the period in which there was a great increase in the numbers who made fortunes or were highly paid following the deregulation of the financial system. Many of them expressed their new wealth by constructing large, extravagant, expensive houses as forms of conspicuous consumption and of tax free investment. There was almost a competition between the newly rich in parading their edifice complexes to see who could construct the greatest excess. It was also a period when executive salary packages rapidly increased, including generous access to housing mortgage finance, which would also have had the effect of increasing house size at the top of the range. Simultaneously there was a boom in house markets, especially in Sydney and Melbourne. The introduction of capital gains taxes on property acquired after 1986, other than the owner occupied family home, encouraged the market boom and the construction of larger houses. The easier availability of finance facilitated these responses.

Table 1.5

Average Size of New Houses

Year	Average Floor Area (square metres)				
	Sydney SD	NSW	Melbourne SD	VIC	Australia
1970	*	*	*	*	130
1971	135	*	132	*	129
1972	138	*	135	*	131
1973	145	*	138	*	135
1974	152	*	148	*	145
1975	153	*	147	*	145
1976	145	*	146	*	141
1983	139	146	179	169	164
1984	146	149	176	167	163
1985	165	161	179	169	166
1986	176	169	184	174	175
1987	188	177	185	176	179
1988	181	177	192	183	184
1989	192	189	235	210	196
1990	182	179	185	179	187
1991	181	180	180	175	186
1992	188	185	176	175	185

Source: 1970 Australia – NHS, *Agenda for Action* 1992; Sydney, NSW, Melbourne, Victoria, Australia 1983–1992, ABS Building Approvals microfiche Tables, 3, 4 and 6 [unpublished data]; 1971-1976 Sydney, Melbourne, Australia – Social Indicators 1978, Table 7.12.

Note: 1983 Sydney Statistical Division and New South Wales – data are for calendar year; all other data are for financial year; 1971–1976 Australia – data are for total of capital city statistical divisions excluding Darwin; 1983–1992 Australia – data are for total of all States; * comparable data not available.

Table 1. 6

Flats, as Percentage of Total Private Occupied Dwellings: Australia, Sydney, Melbourne and Remainder of State

Year		Total Private Occupied Dwellings	Flats & Other Medium Density[a]		Flats & Other Private Dwellings[b]	
		Number	Number	%	Number	%
1971	Australia	3,670,553	492,431	13.4	590,312	16.0
	Sydney SD	845,714	191,733	22.7	217,895	25.8
	Rem NSW	510,797	39,811	7.8	52,256	10.2
	Melb SD	731,687	1,255,011	17.1	140,401	19.2
	Rem VIC	278,499	23,166	8.3	27,179	10.0
1976	Australia	4,140,521	583,866	14.1	805,013	19.4
	Sydney SD	972,826	235,658	24.2	284,532	29.2
	Rem NSW	519,000	35,826	7.0	57,784	11.0
	Melb SD	813,402	148,718	18.3	190,190	23.4
	Rem VIC	30,8176	13196	4.3	23,366	7.6
1981	Australia	4,668,909	733,538	15.7	938,673	20.1
	Sydney SD	1,065,078	278,306	26.1	326,070	30.6
	Rem NSW	597,681	54,469	9.1	73,960	12.4
	Melb SD	851,641	168,256	20.0	204,721	24.0
	Rem VIC	387,305	20,733	5.4	30,266	7.8
1986	Australia	5,264,516	847,767	16.1	1,106,825	21.0
	Sydney SD	1,145,396	301,097	26.3	348,834	30.5
	Rem NSW	687,246	67,639	10.0	103,858	15.1
	Melb SD	960,556	177,247	19.0	213,664	22.2
	Rem VIC	395,679	25,053	6.3	39,948	10.1
1991	Australia	5,642,320	1,063,553	18.9	1,171,846	21.0
	Sydney SD	1,219,682	370,517	30.4	452,692	37.1
	Rem NSW	767,660	94,717	10.1	186,742	24.3
	Melb SD	1,048,988	224,419	21.4	233,145	22.2
	Rem VIC	426,242	35,432	8.3	45,946	10.8

Source: Census of Population and Housing, Australia

Note: (a) Due to changes in census collection methods and classifications the definition of flats etc is not exactly equivalent in the output for all census years Although an attempt has been made here to make this definition as comparable as possible across census years, the resulting figures should be treated as estimates only; (b) 1976–1991 – all categories of occupied private dwellings except 'Separate House' and 'Not Stated'; 1971 – all categories except 'Private House' ('Not Stated' category not tabulated separately in 1971 Census output and Private House classification included row and terrace houses).

Finally, and more importantly, during the period when most of the increase in average house size is alleged to have occurred (from 1984!) State governments changed the regulations covering the construction of *granny flats* by allowing them to be constructed under the dual occupancy policy. Houses were allowed to be constructed with a self contained flat up to 40 per cent of the size of the *main* house. Although some were structurally attached to the *main* house they were often separate structures on the same parcel of land. Only one building permit was required with a single figure for the value of construction and area of building. (Later changes in regulations allowed the issue of separate strata titles for these dwellings.) What appeared in the official statistics for building approvals as one large house was actually two dwellings—one of which was usually relatively small. In some cases the *main* house was itself constructed so that after completion it could also be converted to two self contained flats meaning that, for those cases, the approval figures for large new houses were actually three dwellings. While this had occurred earlier the practice is thought to have increased under the consolidation policy. At present it is not possible to provide an accurate estimate of the average size of new houses built let alone new dwellings, and it is even less feasible to estimate the size of dwellings in the stock.

Over the period cited the proportion of dwellings described as flats increased substantially (Table 1.6). This was due to an increase in the proportion of new dwellings built as flats, the conversion of large houses to flats and the conversion of other buildings such as warehouses to flats (we should note that there has been some reconversion of old terraces and other housing which had been operated as flats and rooming houses back to single family dwellings but the scale of this is not known although it is undoubtedly slight in its impact on average dwelling size). Many of these flats were substitutes for the smaller houses. This point is confirmed if we broaden the definition to include with flats, dwellings described in the census as other medium density, villa units, town houses and row or terrace houses. 'This would have had the effect of reducing the demand for new smaller houses and thereby increasing the apparent *average* for new houses. Because statistics are not collected for these kinds of dwellings the average size of new dwellings would have risen less than the average size of new houses.

The increase in the size of houses is an artefact of the way the statistics about new houses are assembled and a reflection of the changing mix of dwelling types as a result of the *success* of government policy. (It is ironic that in using size of new houses as if it reflected size of dwellings the argument ignores the increase in the supply of smaller dwellings, which is what government policy aims to achieve.)

Note that in Sydney the proportion of occupied private dwellings which are flats has always been much higher than in Australia as a whole or Melbourne. Indeed, throughout the period, all Censuses recorded more than 25 per cent of all occupied private dwellings were other than the *conventional* private house.

But the question remains: So what? It could be argued that the issue of dwelling size is irrelevant. We would expect dwellings to get bigger as living standards rose and people made themselves more comfortable. It is a matter of record that until the mid 1950s households were encouraged by governments to be satisfied with *starter* homes. That is, with houses which were smaller than they desired but which were constructed with the intention of expanding them as the family grew and/or as households could afford it. Commonwealth Government policy was directed at sharing the scarce building materials so that the maximum number of households could be housed in their own homes and on the assumption that the houses could subsequently be expanded. We note in passing that in Europe dwelling sizes, even in the high density stock, increased by 20 to 30 per cent in the 1950s and 1960s while the average household size actually fell (Harloe 1994).

None of the increase in house size is a matter for concern unless the growth is the outcome of distortions in the tax regime or investment incentives, unless it masks a departure from the equitable distribution of housing which had characterised Australian housing until recently or it results in unwelcome environmental consequences. The first minister to draw attention to the statistics relating to the alleged increase in average size of new houses was Peter Walsh when he was Minister for Finance (1988). There is no public evidence that he questioned the validity or appropriateness of the data yet he argued that the implication of this alleged increase in average size of new houses (which he conflated as new dwellings) was that as a nation we were over-investing in housing thereby reducing our competitive position compared with our trading partners. Other ministers, State and Federal, subsequently took similar positions. And the National Housing Strategy re-published the data with no qualifications about its accuracy or relevance.

The figures for new house approvals were given currency as though they represented all dwellings. The inference was that Australians were investing in housing which was far too large for their needs, yet it is clear from the evidence of the distribution of house size that the great majority of citizens built houses which were little different in size at the end of the 1980s compared with those at the beginning of the 1970s. But what is the economic evidence for the Walsh thesis of over-investment? Hendershott and Bourassa (1992) certainly do not support the argument that Australia is generally over-investing compared with its trading partners. They found evidence that only higher income people had an incentive to over-invest but that was a function of the exemption from capital gains tax that personal housing investment receives. It may be supposed that the higher income households invested in larger, more expensive housing.

There could be a case on equity and efficiency grounds for discouraging the construction of very large houses such as those over 250 square metres which so dramatically influenced the *average* for new houses during the 1980s but there is little case for reducing the size of houses for the majority whose new houses have changed little in size over the period. The 1955 Senate Report on Canberra's development recommended that the size of the largest blocks should be reduced rather than that of the smaller blocks—a more equitable response than the current policy of reducing all blocks.

The fact that so much weight has been given in the formulation of housing and urban policy to such unreliable, volatile statistics is a cause for concern. They provide no case for a government policy for a general reduction in dwelling size.

To return to the historical point made earlier, we should not be surprised to discover that the average size of dwelling has increased as living standards had risen. We should simply have pointed to the increase and said it represented an increase in living standards and was evidence of the strength and progress of the Australian economy. At an earlier stage in our history (a decade ago) if the average house size had risen and there was little dispersion in the distribution we would have been pleased to say that this showed how egalitarian we were and that the system was working in the way we wanted.

V National Versus Disaggregated Analysis

It is inappropriate to discuss housing policy as though there was an undifferentiated national demand and market for housing. It should be clear that there are different issues which require different solutions for different regions and for different scales of urban development. We have already seen how the changing proportion of the population which is classified as *rural* and *urban* must affect the way we interpret historical data. The national statistical data are neither consistent in definition over the period under review nor presented in a way which allows for detailed study of the various sub sections or sub markets for housing. The appropriate level of analysis especially for those issues related to urban policy such as consolidation should be directed at the scale of urban centres most likely to be affected. The level of analysis should be the major cities.

We do not explore here the kind of disaggregations which would be ideal. We have already seen from the outline data above (Tables 1.3, 1.5, 1.6) that housing in Sydney is substantially different from that in Melbourne and each differs, from the remainder of its respective State and from the national picture. Moreover, we know that the tenure of dwellings in those cities differ substantially (Troy 1991) reflecting the different history of public policy in their States and the articulation of social values in them. Melbourne for example, has had a higher level of owner occupation than Sydney, ever since settlement.

We should acknowledge that the housing requirements and conditions of those in rural areas are likely to differ from those in smaller urban centres which in turn differ from those in the largest cities. It follows from this that the desired or appropriate policy prescriptions for the largest cities are likely to differ from those for the other major urban centres and the rural areas.

VI Average Size of Block

It is frequently argued that block sizes in urban housing subdivisions are *too large*. The claim is usually in some undefined absolute sense but is meant to imply that the size of the residential blocks has led to increased costs in the provision of services. Reference is made to the *quarter acre block* (approximately 1000 square metres or one-tenth of a hectare) as though that was the standard or average size. The facts, however, do not support this statement and have not done so for some considerable time. Net residential density in terms of dwellings per hectare of new urban development has risen substantially over the postwar period. This result flowed from the success of development control measures which prevented developments which could not be adequately serviced together with more rational development of the infrastructure services—particularly roads, water supply and sewerage. The average block size is now about 700 square metres which is about two-thirds the size claimed. (The median sized new block in Sydney for example is now around 550 square metres). That is, the fall in average block size occurred as a result of the measures adopted by the planning authorities, local governments and service agencies to eliminate *sprawl*—requiring developers to reticulate services had the effect of both *tightening* development and producing smaller blocks.

Because housing occupies only a small proportion of urban land and because people who live in high density housing need more public open space, reducing the average size of residential blocks makes little difference to the area of the city and therefore to the costs of providing infrastructure (Harrison 1970, McLoughlin 1993). McLoughlin illustrated the futility of the argument when he showed that a net residential area the size of Perth would be reduced by only 4500 hectares (McLoughlin 1993) if a density scenario of 45 persons per hectare were adopted instead of a *no change* scenario of 27.5 persons per hectare, yielding a total land take saving of about 1.8 per cent over the *no change* scenario. That is, there is nothing to be gained by overcrowding under present consolidation policies.

VII Loss of Land

One of the concerns of environmentalists is that the alleged *sprawl* of the city results in loss of valuable agricultural lands and the clearance of yet more natural bushland. This is an old argument which has a simple attraction to it. The *loss* of agricultural lands might be a more serious problem if, as in Canada, Australian cities were located on very limited areas of highly productive agricultural land. But that is not the situation. Very little of the land on which the major Australian cities have developed was prime quality fertile agricultural land. Even in Adelaide where substantial areas formerly devoted to vineyards have been covered with urban development, the State has ample supplies of land suitable for viticulture. In any event the assumption that urban land does not produce food is incorrect. If the concern is to protect farmland in order to protect the food supply other policies and techniques are available to serve that end which do not constrain the growth of urban areas. With appropriate encouragement, people living in traditional forms of housing development can make a significant contribution to the production of food in their gardens as occurred in earlier periods. Proper planning of development can be undertaken to protect any valuable farmland which comes under greater threat from the operation of the property market and the attendant speculation in land which is encouraged by weak planning.

Very little urban development takes place on areas newly cleared of natural bushland. Most occurs on land which has already been alienated and has been used for agricultural production or has been subjected to such massive intrusion or impact of settlement that it cannot be regarded as *natural* bushland. Assuming that the concern is to protect bushland or native habitats it seems to this author that other more effective policies and techniques are available to achieve that end than simply trying to constrain urban growth.

Australia has sufficient land for every household which desires it to have a private garden without significant reduction in the land available for farming or for the protection of bushland. That is, there is no need for people to endure a reduction in their standards of space for housing or for their various activities in urban areas.

As has been pointed out above, the density of residential development has little impact on the total area of the city: the form and structure of the city has little effect on the total demand for urban space. The total area required for urban development is largely a function of the total size of the population. Those who wish to restrict the area of Australia covered by urban development of its largest cities should address their arguments to population policy rather than housing and urban development policy. It should be acknowledged, however, that there are some areas where there is little planning control and we now have extensive areas of *rural residential* which do affect the total urbanised area. The development of southeast Queensland, for example, has been characterised by this form of development which leads to poor quality expensive forms of development with many consequential environmental problems. Although these examples rightly attract much critical comment they are the exception and not the norm and should be seen as such when national policies are framed.

If all other space standards besides housing lots were reduced we could see some reduction in the overall land used in a city and therefore in infrastructure costs. But this effectively means, in an economy which responds to market pressures, that the main options are to reduce the space standards for low income housing (because this form of housing is most directly affected by government policy) and for public circulation and recreation (Troy 1992a). In some situations where it has overwhelming power the government may be able to redirect market pressures. It may even be able to get private firms to undertake developments in accordance with its wishes by controlling the provision of services or of manipulation of the land supply. Victorian and New South Wales governments have taken such actions in the new fringe developments of Melbourne and Sydney but it is probably most obvious in Canberra where the Australian Capital Territory government is the monopoly owner of all land for urban development. In Canberra the incoming residents are unhappy with this situation. They face new estates which have little open space, virtually no public facilities, where the schools are provided long after they are developed and where it is difficult to provide garbage collection and bus services (*CT* 1 September 1992). Many of the Green Street developments suffer from the disadvantage of inability to get service vehicles into them. Some observers believe that they are simply recreations of the slum conditions early urban reformers fought to eliminate. We should note too that there remains a strong demand in the market for the more traditional block sizes revealed by the fact that developers continue to advertise their blocks as *full* or *standard* size (*CT* Real Estate section 1992, 1993).

One of the more dramatic examples of the mismatch between government policy and market demands can be seen in many modern housing estates. Government policy has progressively forced a reduction in block sizes yet the demand for spacious housing has continued. The result is that although the average block size has fallen significantly, the average size of new houses in new estates has slowly increased, thus creating suburbs which appear crowded. Larger houses designed to be on spacious blocks and in garden settings are cheek by jowl. The resulting urban space does not meet high design standards and offers much less opportunity for people to extend or improve their dwelling, to landscape their gardens or to grow much of their own food. Cherrybrook and Glenhaven in Sydney are two excellent examples of the poor quality urban development which result from this process.

The present policy has had the perverse result of increasing density of dwellings at the fringe, which is leading to a concentration of low income households at the fringe. This is not an equitable outcome.

VIII Relocation and Transaction Costs

The proposal that households should move to housing more "appropriate to their needs" (meaning smaller dwellings) (NHS1991b) also takes no account of the costs of moving from one dwelling to another. Indeed, many contributions to the debate appear to assume that the moves are costless. There are two kinds of cost: the first is money costs. In the case of owner occupied dwellings these costs include transaction costs: public taxes, estate agent and lawyers' fees which amount to between 7 and 11 per cent of the value of the property being sold.* There are also costs of acquisition—

*This estimate is based on information provided by the Real Estate Institute of Australia (Australian Capital Territory, New South Wales, Victoria offices), the ACT Rental Bonds Office and the ACT Housing Trust.

lawyers fees, mortgage establishment costs where necessary, building inspection fees, and so on. Both owners and renters have relocation costs which include moving and establishment expenses. Governments might claim that they are trying to reduce transfer costs to encourage the move to smaller dwellings by trying to reduce lawyers and estate agents' fees for example, but while stamp duties remain one of the few taxes available to State governments which are unambiguously under their control, it is unlikely that we shall see significant reduction in these costs.

The second kind of cost is that of social dislocation and re-establishment which are no less real than financial costs and may be even more important to the individuals affected and to their communities. The costs may include the wrench from familiar surroundings that the resident(s) themselves have developed using much creative effort and energy. In many cases individuals are understandably loath to move from houses and gardens which they and their partners have jointly improved and tended for many years. If the emotional trauma of moves which are voluntary are significant, those moves which are forced on people are even more difficult. No less significant is the social dislocation which breaks friendships of long standing and mutual support among neighbours. These are often specially important for the elderly who live in many of the *allegedly under-occupied* dwellings. There is ample evidence that these emotional costs are experienced by people moved from their dwellings regardless of their tenure.

In those professions and occupations where people are required to move periodically (banking, teachers, police, members of the defence forces), programs are developed to help them overcome the resulting stresses and to facilitate their re-establishment and integration in their new community. But there seems to be no recognition of these difficulties in the current policies designed to encourage people to move. Arguably, there would be even greater need for support for the people who are the target of such policies because typically they are older and, in some senses, have reduced capacity to re-establish themselves and integrate into new communities.

Efficiency arguments about the need to encourage/force people to move and relocate to smaller dwellings as their household size falls ignore the distribution of benefits and costs of the moves. The benefits from the policy of relocation derive from the alleged public gains from an imagined increase in efficiency in the provision of housing. The central assumption of the policy is that a closer fit between the size distribution of dwellings and the size distribution of households will lead to lower investment in housing and the related infrastructure services which in turn would release funds for investment in other purposes. It is also claimed that there would be benefits to the individuals from anticipated reduced housing costs but these are not quantified. The costs, however, are all borne by the individuals affected and, as indicated above, are considerable. The communities in which the households are allegedly *over-consuming* housing also bear costs in the form of reduced coherence, stability and security when their older citizens move out. There can be no doubt that some older people are better supported and prefer to live in retirement villages and nursing homes but it would seem that the policy priority should be to find ways of supporting older people in the communities in which they have lived until such time that they need or wish to move to supported accommodation.

It is also observable that the prices of the *more appropriate* dwellings are frequently no lower than those of the dwellings vacated so that the *efficiency gain* is at the cost to the mover of earlier payment of transaction costs and taxes. Although it is claimed that the policy is designed to encourage older people who are in dwellings which are allegedly too large for them to move to smaller more appropriate dwellings, most medium density dwellings are not designed with older, less agile or frailer occupants in mind, or they are for the upper end of that market, which they cannot afford.

Moreover, moves to more appropriate housing in the form of retirement villages frequently require a considerable entrance premium and/or a progressive loss of equity in their unit in the village. These latter points often worry older people because they fear a loss of independence and see their capacity to *leave something for their children and grand children* significantly reduced. Some even worry that if they live long enough they may actually not have the resources to remain in the village (we should note in passing that older owners have similar fears about some of the negative mortgage schemes designed to allow them to have access to the asset they hold in the form of their house).

IX Fallacious Propositions

Commentators argue that as the *typical* household no longer has children, it no longer needs the *traditional* three bedroom house for its accommodation. It is implied that as the children leave the family home (for that read *house*) the parents should be prepared to move to a smaller dwelling, allegedly more appropriate to their needs. Much of the government's argument rests on an implicit demographic argument that changes in household size and social relations necessarily require a change in the housing stock.

There are three problems with this kind of argument. The first is that, at best, the censuses give only a picture at a given time from cross-sectional data from which we can construct only an indicative life history; the second is that it is built on a peculiarly mechanistic conception of the family and its life course, and the third is that it rests on a very limited idea of community.

The notion of the typical family life-cycle is conceived as one in which a couple (whether married or not) sets up a home together. This has often been in rented accommodation, frequently in a multi-dwelling structure. It is assumed that the household remains in that kind of accommodation until the first child is born (or shortly after) when it moves out to a house which it has usually bought in the suburbs. Although the household might move within the house market (typically houses with five rooms—three bedrooms) before the children leave home, it is assumed that once the children leave, the household is occupying a house which is too large for it. The further assumption is made that when household members retire they will have a reduced need for housing and that when one partner dies the need will again be reduced.

X Life Course

Instead of a life-cycle approach, Elder (1975, 1985) alerted us of the need to think about life courses in terms of trajectories and transitions and these have special relevance to considerations of demand for housing. Kendig (1990a) argues that the simple static life-cycle approach, which many contemporary policy analysts employ, does not accord well with the life course experience of many households. He makes the point that the way people move through housing changes over time, and occurs within a stock of housing which is itself changing. Kendig shows that although the housing career of an individual is usually an *upward* progression it may also be lateral or *downward.* Indeed, an individual may experience a series of transitions which take them *up, down* or *sideways* at different stages in their life course. An individual may leave the parental home but return to it, enter owner occupation but then move to rental accommodation, establish a home with another person, leave, then establish a home with the same or another person at a later period.

The permutations and combinations are as varied as the people concerned. Under these circumstances it is inappropriate to use essentially cross-sectional data about the household distribution at different periods to formulate policy relating to or affecting the housing trajectory of individuals. The evidence of Anderton & Lloyd (nd) shows that increasingly children are returning to live with their parents after even quite long periods away. Why these moves occur is an interesting research question but some part of it is due to changing economic fortunes and prospects of the young and changes in attitudes to sexual and social behaviour of both the young and their parents.

There are two further inconvenient points: first, the sequential life-cycle approach employed takes no account of the historical fact that individuals have tended to consume more rather than less housing to make themselves more comfortable as their discretionary income and wealth has risen and the cost of child raising has fallen; and, secondly it takes little account of how individuals use the space in and around their dwellings. For example, the simple assumption that because the children have left home the remaining household does not need the space *freed* ignores the way households actually use the space for return visits by the children and their households, by grandchildren and other relatives, by friends and for a rich miscellany of activities, hobbies and pursuits of the individuals in the household.

The assumption that when people retire they will have a reduced need for housing is also inconsistent with the actual behaviour of households. Note that the fact that older people spend more time in and around their homes is confirmed by insurance companies which set lower insurance premiums for house and contents for those over 55. Indeed, if the policy analysts had their way, individuals would be forced to occupy smaller dwellings precisely at the point when they begin to spend a greater proportion of their time in and around their homes and need the extra space. The increasing incidence of individuals retiring at younger ages will tend to increase the numbers of households which spend the greater part of their life in and around the home. In addition in an increasing proportion of households a member has been retrenched in middle age and faces the prospect of long periods of unemployment.

There is strong evidence that the recreational activities of older people are mostly in or around the house and garden (Davison, Kendig, Stephens & Merrill 1993). The increased numbers living to old age will probably mean an increase in the demand for housing and garden space rather than less. Grahn (nd) makes the point that exercise in the garden is an aid to the health of households especially of older citizens. He points out that it is extremely important for their continued psychic health that they have contact with a type of environment with which they have already established a relationship—that is, moving them to dwellings without gardens may not be beneficial to their continued health.

It is clear that some households do want to reduce their housing consumption when the house and garden is too large for them. This may be a special need for some who are too frail but it should be acknowledged that the need for many is not to move into a smaller independent dwelling but to move to a retirement *village* or supported accommodation. In any event it is illogical to fashion policy on the assumption that all older people should move to the smaller higher density housing proposed. Kendig has written authoritatively (1984a, 1984b, 1990a, 1990b) on the housing needs and preferences of the aged but his evidence and arguments have been given little weight in recent policy debates.

It is even more illogical to use the assumption that older people should move to smaller, higher density housing to justify the wholesale conversion of the housing stock to meet what *at best* is a short term requirement of a small proportion of households. The position that *all* housing must be permitted to have a *granny flat* built in the backyard or to be converted to dual occupancy lacks a logical base and will result only in the creation of extensive areas with little diversity and low levels of amenity.

XI Community

The model of community implicit in current housing and urban development policy assumes that people change their housing every time their household circumstances change whereas the more popularly held idea of community implicit in other areas of policy assumes a high degree of stability and continuity.

Hopkins (1994:1) argues that "[C]ommunity is the basis of our very identity, both individual and collective". This may slightly overstate the realities of urban life in Australia but it summarises the popular perception of community and helps explain why households resist the arguments based on notions of economic efficiency which inform consolidation policy. The struggles to provide or retain facilities for the local school, recreation facilities, a post office branch or something as small as a bus stop or pedestrian crossing reflect the willingness of residents of particular areas to become organised. The shared experiences in developing gardens in a new area; the neighbourly acts of looking after pets, child minding, watching out for neighbours' property, collecting the mail while neighbours are away, sharing garden produce—all the little kindnesses and considerations which are the flux of social existence; the confidence which grows from familiarity with the physical environment and with the people who live in it and their institutions all contribute to a notion of community which individuals want to retain. The shared identification in cultural expression also helps develop a sense of identity which reinforces the notion of community. It may not mean they are prepared to take joint action on major issues but it confers some sense of continuity, stability and security which they value.

The crude physical determinism implicit in the romantic image projected by proponents of higher density housing that it will produce a stronger sense of community and that people will discover the virtues of neighbourliness and become more caring and sharing is inconsistent with the realities of urban living. Paradoxically, people are expected *to keep themselves to themselves*—to have a high degree of independence yet maintain a sense of social or communal engagement. It is easier to achieve both independence and engagement with one's neighbours in conventional housing. To the extent that higher density housing affects community we would have to conclude that it creates the conditions for socially deviant behaviour, isolation and anomie as people act to preserve their privacy and personal space. Rather than encourage engagement, high density housing is more likely to provide the conditions for anonymity and withdrawal. In a society which has fostered individualism and reduced emphasis on collective consumption and supports separatism, the idea that increasing density will cause people to be more concerned with and benevolent towards their fellow citizens seems somewhat fanciful. A sense of community is more deeply a function of the way we value the unity, integrity and equality of the development of our culture than of propinquity or geographical boundaries.

The research into earlier attempts to introduce high density housing both in Australia and overseas found evidence that it had a detrimental effect on household life and particularly on the health of children (Stevenson et al 1967). Much of this research was into high rise high density housing but the central points were that high density housing was synonymous with low levels of privacy and provision of community facilities and services, that the high density housing militated against households exercising appropriate supervision of children and that high density housing gave households little choice or flexibility in their home-based activities. We have no comparable research on the modern low rise high density housing which is resulting from the present policies but we must expect that, to the extent that physical conditions affect people's lives, similar low levels of privacy, services and facilities and similar spatial constraints on home-based activities will tend to reproduce similar stresses and similar evidence of alienation and anomie among households from similar socio-economic backgrounds. The survey evidence of low rise high density housing in Mount Druitt in Sydney and Broadmeadows in Melbourne indicates that that form of housing is deficient in terms of public/private boundaries and visibility/safety in the view of its residents (Peel 1995).

The attempts early in the twentieth century to provide more parks and gardens in cities grew out of a strong conviction that developments which had more open space in the form of private and public gardens were healthier. There was little empirical evidence then to support the contention. More recently, however, the connection between parks and gardens (especially trees and shrubs) and individual and community health has been established. These health effects are derived not only from the outdoor exercise effects but from the beneficial effect of gardens on psychic health as well. Young children have better development as a result of their contact with the natural world. Those who have their own gardens suffer tiredness only 42 per cent as often as those who live in blocks of flats without balconies. Those with gardens of more than 600 square metres have the discomfort of stress only half as often as those who live in flats without balconies. Households with a garden or park close at hand are more likely to have a high level of outdoor use whereas their usage of outdoor areas falls rapidly with distance. Households 500 metres from a park use it 56 per cent less than those near it and those 300 metres away use it 26 per cent less (Grahn nd).

The cleaning effect that trees have on air pollution both in taking up CO_2 and in removing particulates is a major reason private and public garden space should be preserved. That is, on grounds of improved public health and increased amenity the policy should be to preserve traditional density development rather than destroy it by reducing lot sizes and public open space standards for some imagined short-term gain.

XII Lack of Choice

A major issue in the policy debate has been the argument that people have too narrow a choice among different kinds of housing. Much of the argument rests on the claim that individuals find themselves in housing which they believe is too large for their household and that they would move to smaller dwellings if there was a *better* choice; that their housing is poorly designed and that they would choose better designed dwellings if they were available. But what is the evidence? The argument embodies a peculiarly physical determinist perspective. It implies that households cannot, will not or do not want to utilise the extra space they have when all the evidence is that they do and that they *expand* to fill the space available to them. It also implies that developers have failed to supply appropriately sized housing. But there are dwellings of a wide variety of sizes and design in large cities, and if developers believe there is a gap in the offerings they can fill it profitably. There is no evidence of such a gap.

Apart from the motherhood statement that people should have more of it the arguments about choice seem to reduce to five questions: issues of dwelling size, dwelling type, design, location and housing tenure.

1 Dwelling size

Whether we explore the issue of choice of dwelling size by examining statements of preference or whether we explore the preference as revealed in the market we have to conclude that the great majority of the population desires and has always wanted larger rather than smaller dwellings. They are constrained by their ability to pay, and as their real incomes rise that constraint is gradually relaxed. Historically part of the increase in standard of living enjoyed by the population has been reflected in the increased consumption of housing. A great part of the additions and alterations to the housing stock is undertaken by households which seek to modernise and extend their housing to suit their needs and their pockets. They will often decide to extend and alter their houses rather than move, even when, in narrow economic terms, it might be more advantageous for them to do so—because they *like the area* or community.

The argument about increased choice in dwelling size rests on the claim that there is too little variation in the size of dwellings. It is argued that the fact that the conventional/traditional house which has three bedrooms or flat which has two bedrooms (see Table 1.4) offers limited choices to the public. There seems little recognition in this argument that this size of dwelling is the market response to demand and that, in any event, it provides most occupants with the flexibility in their living arrangements and activities they desire. If none, or a very few were being built there may be an argument for excessive supply, but they are being built. In some locations supply may shape demand although many developers and housing financiers would respond by saying that the housing they supply is simply a prudent response to demand.

2 Dwelling type

This raises a difficult set of issues. The argument about choice does not usually focus on issues of architectural style but consideration of questions of style-as-fashion are intimately involved.

If we look at the historical progression in dwelling types several points emerge: the progression from terrace and tenement houses to separate bungalows on their own block of land as the dominant dwelling type was initially influenced by prevailing ideas and a number of developments in Australian cities. These included the need for households to produce much of their own food, easy availability of land, prevailing ideas about the transmission of disease, the healthiness of houses in their own gardens compared with high density housing, physical determinist and eugenic notions of social reform and the development of public transport. Later the availability of reticulated water and sewerage and notions of modernity and fashion helped continue the trend. More recently the increase in car ownership helped maintain it (Mullins 1987, Reiger 1985, 1991).

One of the reasons households prefer traditional houses is that they meet their desire for a separate front and back door and for some private outdoor space. The space available to a household enables it to invest in its own symbolism. Households living in houses can *present* themselves to the world in a manner of their own choosing free from confusion over the signals which a single door gives. They can determine how they will show their public face and they can maintain a more intimate private face at the back door which is shown more to close friends and family.

3 Dwelling design

The NHS report on housing choice (NHS 1992b) discusses issues of design leaving the clear impression that in some way it is only limited design choice which governs the acceptance of innovation. This ignores the fact that the issue was first raised by the Commonwealth Housing Commission which reported in 1944 and for many years the Commonwealth, through its Building Research and Development Advisory Council, itself pursued an extensive education program based on a vigorous research and development program to encourage people to apply scientific advances in the design of dwellings and the incorporation in them of energy saving design and equipment. This program was directed to the public, professional designers such as architects, builders and developers. It did not have great success. The conservatism of the finance industry, including the banks, militated against innovation in housing. Similar conservatism is thought to be prevalent among real estate agents, builders and local government authorities. We can be sympathetic to the desire to improve design but it is necessary to be realistic about the probability of success. There is also conservatism among buyers concerned about the resale value of their property. Greig's *The Stuff Dreams Are Made Of* (1995) gives a fuller account of the shifting fashions in designing the Australian house (home) of the 1950s and the limited impact of modernism.

One aspect of design choice which has been contentious relates to the material of the outside walls of the dwellings. Most would nowadays agree that the prejudice against timber walled dwellings is unfortunate and the preference for *full brick* over *brick veneer* might be irrational if we gave serious consideration to the energy efficiency of dwellings. But the influence of fashion and the conservatism of buyers and local authorities serves to entrench the view that full brick housing is superior in quality.

We should also note that there has been a significant increase in the number of households living in caravans and *relocatable* homes (Mowbray 1994). Recent changes in the law and regulations covering caravans and relocatable homes, especially in New South Wales, have been designed to increase the security and social acceptability of this form of accommodation on the grounds that it increases choice of housing. This form of housing is expensive in terms of its unit cost, has a high rate of depreciation and usually incurs significant weekly site rentals and has many social disadvantages including loss of privacy and autonomy, which Mowbray discusses. Acceptance of this kind of housing must be seen as a result of governments failing to meet their traditional obligation to house those who cannot afford appropriate housing provided by the market. As incomes rise it is likely to be stigmatised like other kinds of *slums*.

We know that the overwhelming majority of households living in houses are happy with their choice of dwelling, we also know that a significant majority of those who live in flats would prefer to live in houses. We could conclude from this that the choice people have is limited—that we should build more rather than fewer houses and help the lower income people to afford them. This is the opposite of the consolidation policy.

But *design* raises another set of issues. There are some who hold the view that if only we could produce better design we would avoid or alleviate many of the alleged problems of urban development. It is true that buildings are often not well located in relation to their neighbours, are poorly oriented to the sun or prevailing winds, are built with materials which are unsympathetic to one another or the climate, are out of scale with people and with one another or have poor circulation within or between them. But this does not provide a case for higher density.

Frequently the critics of the design of suburbs of Australian cities imply that higher density development would be of a higher aesthetic standard with a greater level of amenity. However, no analysis is presented to support this assertion and the aesthetic poverty of much of the existing higher density development does not support it. There seems to be an overweening desire on the part of proponents of consolidation to *educate* people, to change their preferences, to *lead* the unwilling citizenry into higher densities. It is hard to escape the conclusion that much of the medium density development that professionals decide is *good* design is not so regarded by the general public or even the residents of the *approved* developments.

Many of the urban developments in other countries held up as examples of high quality design were carried out by dictators or people with near absolute control. They were usually carried out in cities which were much smaller and in periods when the technological constraints on the scale and nature of development meant that buildings could not be very tall and in areas where the development was under one ownership. In Australia, where there is a highly fragmented ownership of property, virtually no technological constraints on scale and a high degree of choice, the idea that there should be some kind of czar of taste and design who should decide what buildings should be built, where and with what materials and having some kind of aesthetic relationship with one another is anathema to the public. The political realities are that control of design raises insuperable problems going to the heart of the rights of individual owners of property and it would be literally impossible for one person to be able to give permission for a particular development given the multiplicity of services with which each development needs to be connected. This becomes more difficult the more the service agencies are corporatised or privatised. As much as observers might complain about poor quality design little can be done about it in situations where individuals have a choice of materials and kind of building.

Another feature of the preoccupation with *design* is that most contributors to the debate, especially those who deplore the tastes of lower income households, ignore the dynamic nature of the issue. They seem to forget that what might be judged good *design* today might not be tomorrow; that what is judged to be good design is as much an issue of fashion and a reflection of the vales and attitudes of a dominant group as it is about the intrinsic qualities of a building or space. This is not to say that design is not important—it is—but it is more a question of education and persuasion than the introduction of *enlightened* autocratic control.

4 Issues of location

Most people choose where to live because, within their means, the dwelling location and its location best meets their needs. Much of the policy debate is, however, predicated on the assumption that people seek or should seek good access to the centre of the city and that they are frustrated from making their preferred location choices by the present form of the city. The choices people make of where to live, work, shop and to pursue their cultural and recreational interests suggest that the city they experience is not highly centralised. Their choices are of course constrained by the centralised transport systems and the inherited central location of major institutions but it is clear that most of their activities focus on *sets* of sub centres within the metropolitan area. This suggests that their location choices are influenced by considerations of urban structure rather than form.

A little less than one in five people in the workforce living in Australian cities work in the city centre, about a third work in the local government area in which they live and work destinations of the remainder are distributed throughout the metropolitan area. Data from the Housing and Location Choice Study (HALCS) suggest that although as many as a third of Sydney households find their dwelling is poorly located in relation to the city centre, no more than one in six think that it is important to have convenient access to the city centre. In Melbourne and Adelaide fewer find themselves inconveniently located relative to the city centre and fewer think it is important to be so conveniently located (Edwards & Madden 1991). The same surveys indicate greater concern by residents about their access to cultural and recreational facilities and services—evidence which supports the data on trips and travel. Research by Maher et al (1992) confirms that people who live in the suburbs do not perceive themselves to be locationally disadvantaged. This contemporary research tends to confirm the research into perceptions of environmental quality carried out in Sydney and Melbourne 25 years ago (Troy 1971, 1972). That research showed that although people had some complaints about specific features of their location and environment, on the whole they tended to be very satisfied with their location and their dwellings which suggests that they have made the choices in their location which best meet their demands, given their resources.

There is no reason for policy makers to assume that the market will always satisfy people's housing and locational choices but neither is it appropriate to use policy to limit location choice under the guise of increasing it. Early indications of the outcomes of the market response to consolidation are that it results in greater isolation of low-income households by forcing more of them to outer suburban locations. Government housing programs focusing on constructing medium density housing on the fringe actually increases disadvantage of the outer suburbs.

5 Housing tenure

The argument that present housing policy offers people little choice in their tenure raises interesting questions. In their study of home ownership among postwar Australian cohorts, Neutze and Kendig (1991) found that approximately 92 per cent of people own a dwelling at some stage in their life and that almost 85 per cent continue to own until near the end of their lives. We know that at any given time over the past 30 years approximately 70 per cent of households owned or were purchasing their own dwelling (various censuses). There is substantial historical evidence that home ownership was regarded as one of the distinguishing features of Australian society and that it was a state to which *the ordinary working man* could reasonably aspire. Stretton (1974) argued that postwar policies of fostering home ownership gave low income households a chance to share in the bounty of the nation. Recent work by Stevens, Baum and Hassan (1992) confirms that home ownership remains the preferred tenure for Adelaide residents and the HALCS survey confirms this for Sydney and Melbourne.

The weight of this evidence suggests that the benefits (economic as well as non-economic) of owner occupation are substantial (Troy 1991), that people understand this and that their aspirations in this direction are likely to remain strong over the foreseeable future. In this case notions of increasing *tenure choice,* if it means reducing owner occupation, do not appear consistent with community expectations and desires.

The encouragement of a high level of owner occupation is a major element of the notion of domestic defence which is central to the development of the welfare state in Australia (Castles 1994). Any withdrawal from owner occupation necessarily raises the issue of what compensatory measures will be introduced to modify the welfare state and to ensure that the level of security which the community desires can be achieved with other forms of tenure. Ideological purists might argue that other forms of tenure are needed and even desired but the evidence both within Australia and overseas suggests that owner occupation is increasingly popular and may even become more valued as a way of delivering security in a world which is otherwise increasingly insecure.

We note, however, that owner occupation has fallen recently and that the fall is greatest among the younger households (Bourassa 1993). This is a tenure choice which is influenced more by their difficulty in obtaining secure jobs and therefore their capacity to take out a mortgage than any decline in the preference for ownership.

We can of course establish no relationship between the strength of the desire for owner occupation and forms of housing. The owner occupancy rate of flat dwellers is lower than that of house dwellers but introducing policies to increase the supply of flats in the belief that this will reduce owner occupancy rates and thereby increase the tenure choice is misguided. Forms of tenure other than owner occupation will only prove attractive if they increase the security of residents. There is little evidence that such forms have been or are being developed. To talk then of the need for increasing tenure choice without indicating what it might mean or how it might be achieved is simply empty rhetoric.

There is no doubt that we value choice, diversity and innovation in a wide range of our activities and pursuits and some argue that it is fundamental to our survival, that we want change but not too much of it (Scitovsky 1976, 1986). But, paradoxically, we also are slaves to fashion and convention and we seem to desire tradition and continuity and the comfort derived from familiarity. It is hard to escape the conclusion that much of the contemporary argument about the lack of choice in Australian housing is a manufactured controversy and much of it is an implied criticism of people's choice of houses over flats. Both the survey evidence and the revealed preferences of people indicate strong preference for single family houses in their own gardens, for owner occupation over renting or other forms of tenure and for a decentralised structure of cities over the highly centralised structure implicit in current housing and urban policy.

Contemporary Commonwealth housing policy has been formulated with little acknowledgment that people find the traditional form of housing to be extremely flexible allowing them a wide variety of choices in living arrangements and cultural and recreational activities for a very long period in their life, a point made by the Industry Commission report on Public Housing in 1993. People have been giving clear indications of their choices, yet government policy is designed to pursue directions diametrically opposed to them. We could conclude that providing there is not too much confusion, choice is good and that there already is enough of it!

The paradox is that the vigorous enforcement of consolidation policies, including allowing dual occupancy, actually is leading to reduction of choice. Suburbs which have experienced extensive development of medium density housing and those which have been the focus of dual occupancy development now have less choice than they did. Blacktown in Sydney, for example, has had a lot of dual occupancy development on *new* subdivisions which has resulted in whole streets being developed as dual occupancy. Dual occupancy dwellings have gone from one unit to 32 detached houses in 1987 to one unit to 2.7 houses in 1993 (Driscoll 1994). The total development approvals for medium density housing in the form of townhouses, cluster or integrated housing, aged person's housing and flats have approximately equalled that of conventional single detached houses since 1988. That is, the choice of housing in that area is now constrained.

XIII Reduction in Housing Costs

A major justification offered for the proposed change to a higher density form of development is that it will reduce housing costs (NHS 1991b). But all the evidence suggests that increasing density—especially to multi-unit construction—will actually lead to increased unit costs (Department of Industry Technology and Commerce (DITAC) 1991a; Scott Carver Pty Ltd 1992; Woodhead 1991). The major reasons for this are related to the differences in institutional and financial arrangements for multi-unit housing compared with the traditional bungalow. It is also more environmentally intrusive and therefore needs more careful consideration.

Multi-unit housing construction, especially if it is more than one storey high, usually has higher overheads due to the scale and complexity of the development and the need to engage more professional skills in the design and construction of the project; and higher cost due to the different structural requirements. Such projects frequently have to be completed in their entirety before they can be used as accommodation; they are hard to develop and occupy in stages which means that developers must raise construction finance on the open market to complete the project. This tends to increase holding costs. Until recently few multi-unit dwellings were sold *off plan* although this is now changing. Even where they are sold off plan, the developer rarely has access to the funds until the whole project is completed. However, few single family houses are built *on spec*, they are usually sold before work commences with payments made as the house is built with the result that the bungalow developer has his investment financed by the purchaser (Australian Housing Industry Development Council (AHIDC) 1991). This means that the purchaser pays the cost of the finance for the period of construction but this period is typically shorter than the time to construct multi-storey dwellings and in any event is at the interest rate for the house mortgage. A second factor relates to the need for greater investment in *hard standing*, site development or paving, and in sound insulation to ensure privacy for the higher density housing thus leading to higher unit costs.

A recent study (AHIDC 1994a, 1994b) of the difference in costs between conventional housing and the higher density forms of development concluded that the costs were higher on the higher density housing because of higher labour costs and higher overhead costs including those due to the longer time taken for the community consideration of the higher density proposals. The longer time required to consider high density proposals arises because they have greater and more varied impact on neighbours. Predictably, the reports proposed reducing labour costs by reducing the working conditions of the more unionised labour used on higher density developments, lowering building standards and speeding up the community consideration of higher density developments. The fact that labour costs on medium density housing are often higher because of the double handling of materials seems to have been overlooked. That is, the *benefit* of reduced costs on higher density housing were to be obtained at the expense of working conditions, reduced standards and less community involvement. The lower costs of conventional housing are also due to the fact that the cottage building industry relies heavily on non-union sub contractors for on-site work.

XIV Lifestyle Choices

The comment that the traditional form of housing does not offer sufficient variety of lifestyles is one of those curious propositions which gain currency but which are little explored. At its heart commentators seem to be saying that living at high density is in some way richer and more enriching; that high density living is more cultured and relaxed. The model seems to be related to an elitist urban life style in which individuals eat out, engage in the pursuits of a romanticised cafe society, have the time to enjoy morning coffee over the newspaper, explore the antique shops, bookshops and art galleries.

Enjoyable as these activities are, they are not the daily options or desires of the overwhelming majority of the population. The proliferation of coffee shops, bistros, restaurants and sidewalk cafes in parts of most of our cities over recent years is a response to changing social behaviour, increasing affluence, the commodification of leisure and to the needs of tourists (both domestic and international) but most of us use them only on special occasions or as part of our recreation. Our use of such services and venues, however attractive and desirable, is more contingent on levels of disposable income and *free* time than on location and form. For all the yearning by some commentators and policy advisers to return to some halcyon past, such urban life styles never were the daily life experience of more than a small minority. Indeed, as Brown-May (1995) shows us in his study of Melbourne, a vibrant street life has not always been regarded as an attractive feature of Australian cities. The street gangs (and their associated territorial disputes) now evident in some North American cities mostly come from high density environments but proponents of high density presumably do not wish to argue that they are a result of density.

Although some Australian cities are large and cosmopolitan enough to provide choices in urban public life, and do, the great majority of households seek outlets for their interests, hobbies and activities in and around their dwellings in our cities. Moreover, there does not seem to be a great unmet demand for more space for so-called urban lifestyle.

The urban life model seems to be founded more on the tourist's impressions and novelty of urban living in the tiny attractive corners of the cities they visit rather than any fair or rigorous exploration of the realities of life for the majority of people in those same cities. More than that, however, the model is built on a crude form of physical determinism—the form of housing does not encourage individuals into frequenting cafes, unless their housing is so cramped that the cafes effectively function as their living space. Whether people eat out and visit art galleries and antique shops is more closely related to their disposable income and their range of cultural interests than to their accommodation arrangements. We should also acknowledge that some part of the appearance of an urban lifestyle reflected in the numbers of men who seem to spend time in cafes or on the side walks nearby in some areas of Australian cities is indicative of a set of gender relations which we might not wish to foster—many of the men are *free* to enjoy that kind of behaviour because their wives are preoccupied with household chores including care and supervision of children. It may be indicative of the behaviour of *first generation* migrants who still behave as they typically would have in their original country but we cannot assume that their children brought up in Australia will have the same set of values.

Implicit in the notion that high density housing leads to a more urban lifestyle is the proposition that behaviour can simply be imported so long as we create the physical setting. None of the proponents of this imagined urban lifestyle provide a social analysis of who actually lives in the manner they yearn for or any historical explanation of the social and cultural processes which produced it. Nor is there much evidence to support the proposition that higher density living leads to greater creativity or higher levels of cultural expression. We would be hard pressed to explain the success of the majority of Australian writers, painters, singers, musicians, intellectuals or even political leaders were that the case.

There are those who complain that the suburbs provide few opportunities for the social life of teenagers. It is undoubtedly true that some people, young and old, find that some of the suburbs are limited in their range of opportunities for the pursuit of their cultural and social interests, but the response should be to explore cultural policy and the way facilities and services are provided rather than simply assume that a change in the form of the city will rectify the perceived shortcomings.

One of the *problems* cities face is that in areas of cultural policy, as in many other areas, a highly centralised approach is taken to the development of publicly funded cultural facilities. There is only one major publicly funded art gallery for example in Sydney and that is in the city centre and not very accessible by public transport. The National Gallery in Melbourne is similarly central but is more accessible by public transport. I do not mean to imply that provision of publicly funded art galleries is all that there is to cultural policy. The provision of publicly funded art galleries is undoubtedly an important component of cultural policy. The point being made here is that an integrated cultural policy would lead to the development of a variety of facilities, venues and services throughout the city, including the suburbs, giving all people, including teenagers, access to venues and events which enrich their cultural and social lives and allow and encourage individual fulfilment and self-expression. Such a policy would be independent of urban form. It might be affected by city structure but this would not necessarily mean it should be highly centralised.

By and large the suburbs, especially the newer ones, have sufficient playing fields for a wide range of organised sports. But any parent who has heard teenagers complain that "[T]here is nothing to do" in their free time quickly realises that they do not mean sport. Nor do they mean there are not enough opportunities to engage in art and craft or other hobby groups.

When parents of teenagers in high and low density areas of large cities or in country towns in Australia hear the same complaint and when they know that similar complaints are made by teenagers from societies in countries as diverse as Australia, England, France and the United States they look for some explanation other than housing density.

Interpreting what teenagers (or even adults) mean when they complain of lack of choice of things to *do* is difficult. Teenagers may simply mean that they have not enough pocket money left to attend a film, disco, band or spectator sport such as basketball of an evening or weekend or visit some favoured cafe or milk bar to *hang out* where their parents are not in control. They may be making an observation about the alienating nature of modern society, the commodification of cultural activities, the passivity of film and television and the homogenised pap those media project, their need to express their independence or simply their need to make contact with others of the same generation. Of course, one explanation of the contemporary fact that some of the city streets are occupied at night by groups of young people who may be perceived to be threatening to others and a danger to themselves is that the dwellings they come from may have insufficient space for them to have privacy.

We are not here engaged in an exploration of social behaviour. Suffice it to say that the complaints about social opportunities and activities should not be interpreted solely or even significantly as related to the form of development. Nor does it follow that to meet the complaints we should redevelop our cities to higher densities. Propinquity may increase the likelihood of social contact but we also know that at high density people act to preserve their personal space and privacy, that is, they withdraw from contact with others or try to limit interactions. We simply do not know whether higher density will eliminate the complaint of lack of choice of activities. If it would we do not know what density will produce the felicitous trade-off between all the other interests households have at different stages in the life courses of their members.

The notion that the form of development can make up for all the other aspects of Australian urban society which lead to people feeling unfulfilled in some way is expecting too much of the urban environment. One way of addressing the issue of alleged alienation would be to provide facilities closer to where young people live, not try to move the young people to where the facilities are. The way households vote through the market expressing preference for traditional forms of housing could be taken as *prima facie* evidence that it best meets their needs for most of the time.

Chapter 2

INFRASTRUCTURE AND HOUSING COSTS

The debate on housing policy has been broadly conceived as being concerned with issues of land and infrastructure development. Claims have repeatedly been made that infrastructure servicing costs are excessive, a burden on the general revenue and could be greatly reduced by reducing block sizes and changing urban form, in particular by increasing density. It is also claimed that the existing infrastructure services have substantial spare capacity and that infrastructure standards are too high and that we cannot afford them.

Table 2.1 sets out a brief analysis of the major reports which have been made in Australia over the past decade on the infrastructure costs for housing development. The reports were commissioned for different purposes and employed different approaches yet they are the source of most of the figures cited as the costs of provision of infrastructure to service the typical housing subdivision. It will be apparent from Table 2.1 that the figures vary widely. This alone should be enough for caution.

An important point about these estimates is that they are not all on the same basis—some include pipe and wire services as well as social services and facilities, they add public and private costs, they include capital and annual costs and capitalised benefits to individuals such as the estimated value of travel time savings as costs. The Neilson report for example attempted to place a value on the net community benefit of consolidation for the Melbourne City Council which at the time (1987) was trying to make the case for preferential development of its area. Over two-thirds of the alleged benefit of $41,640 per household was the private benefit from reduced travel yet the figures have been frequently asserted as the benefit from savings in infrastructure investment. The estimate was highly sensitive to assumptions about where household members worked or went to school. A central implicit assumption was that people would work in the CBD and that children would travel to the nearest government school and by public transport.

Table 2.1 Infrastructure Costs for Housing Development: Fringe Area Development/Existing Residential Area Development

Study title	Net Community Benefits of Urban Consolidation	Public Sector Cost Savings of Urban Consolidation	Financing Urban Infrastructure: Equity and Efficiency Considerations	The Efficient Supply of Affordable Land and Housing: The Urban Challenge	Housing Costs Study Vol 2, Evaluation of Fringe Development and Urban Consolidation
Author	Neilson Associates Pty Ltd	Dwyer/Leslie Pty Ltd Hughes Truman Ludlow	Richard Kirwan Urban Policy Associates Pty Ltd	National Housing Strategy	Travers Morgan Pty Ltd Applied Economics Pty Ltd
Date	Nov 1987	February 1991	1991	1991	February 1991
Commissioned by	Melbourne City Council	Dept of Planning-NSW	Prime Minister and Cabinet	Dept of Health, Housing and Community Services	Australian Building Research Grants Scheme
Purpose	examine likely costs and benefits of increasing residential provision in the City of Melbourne and the inner ring suburbs ie *net community benefit*	ascertain whether there are *public sector physical infrastructure* cost savings in urban consolidation compared with urban development on the fringe	review efficiency and equity implications of some of the options for financing urban infrastructure available to governments and public authorities	to examine how to supply efficient and affordable housing	compare the social benefits and costs of development in fringe areas and urban consolidation in three cities (Melbourne, Sydney, Adelaide)
Approach	Planning Balance Sheet (modified Travers Morgan approach-1986 study) using capital costs and recurrent cost savings	develop a 'model' fringe area without infrastructure and compare cost of servicing this area with cost of augmenting existing services for the consolidation case on a per dwelling or per person basis; physical infrastructure funded by the public sector is then deducted from the total physical infrastructure costs to identify public budget savings from urban consolidation	discussion paper drawing on selected data specifically reviewing options for the financing of urban infrastructure	issues paper canvassing ideas to improve the efficient supply of housing	estimated total net social benefits(total benefits less total costs)of urban consolidation compared with alternatives total net social benefits are equivalent to the sum of the changes in consumer and producer surpluses(or deficits). *components considered*: users of new housing, producers of housing land owners, producers of housing infrastructure services, producers of\ social services for residents, -costs and benefits of other households
Assumptions	a particular structure of the incoming population and households a notional settlement pattern in a metropolitan area for accommodating new	consolidation scenarios established at the metropolitan scale to test public transport and main road differences between consolidation and fringe development	*	*	*fringe*: assumed occupancy rate 3.2 persons per household where the gross density is 10 dw/ha & 3.5 persons/hh where gross density is 8 dw/ha *medium density urban consolidation*: assumed occupancy rate 2.2 persons

Variables Included	*public utilities:* -water supply, drainage, sewerage, electricity, telephone, road provision, private transport education community facilities sport & recreation urban maintenance	*fringe:* hydraulic services: (water, sewerage, storm drainage), utility services (electricity, gas, telephone), roads, public transport *consolidation:* (connection costs, augmentation costs where applicable)		sewer, water drainage, roads, power, telephone, site preparation, survey and design, community facilities such as sport and recreation facilities, police, education, health, ambulance and fire stations.	[illegible] development costs from study one, opportunity cost of land, water, sewerage, drainage, gas, telephone, electricity authorities, road, public transport, health, education, and community services (where avail[illegible]
Cost Estimates	average economic and financial *benefit to the community of $41,640 per household* for an inner versus a fringe residential location (1986/1987 prices) *net community benefits from urban consolidation:* public utilities $8580, travel $27620, education $4040, community facilities and maintenance $1400	cost savings per lot range between *$28,900 –$30,700* (fringe subdivision of average lot size 840m^2 with 18 dw/ha) & *$17,000–$18,900* (fringe subdivision of average lot size 450m^2 with 18 dw/ha)- 1989/1990 prices *cost savings at $30,700*: sewer $8422; water $4171; stormwater $7276; gas $1753; power $2248; telecom $1031; local roads $4635; miscellaneous $1148	no conclusions on this issue	Table 4.1 showing indicative development cost per allotment : fringe land - *average $50,800* with 41% recovered per lot with the balance of $22,500 payable by public sector per lot (source: NCPA amended)	proposed fringe development produces a *net social deficit* of $26m (Syd), $241m (Melb) and a *net social surplus* in Adelaide of $48m in contrast the combined strategy of fringe and urban consolidation (middle suburbs) produces a total *net surplus* of $127m in Sydney and a reduced *net deficit* of $61m in Melbourne
Relevant Conclusions	benefits overall calculated for four different scenarios will be largely dependant on achieving the target densities highest level of quantifiable benefits are associated with two income households with children	potential cost savings of up to $30,700 ($14,100 to the public sector) Qualifications: (a)physical infrastucture capital costs only; (b)ways will need to be found of actually realising the potential reductions in fringe works and translating the potential savings into lower prices for medium density housing; (c)requires active pursuit of density targets by government to achieve savings (note: at that stage achieving half of target in metrop strategy)	planning agencies and infrastructure providers should be encouraged to work out the implications for infrastructure provision and financing of the pursuit of policies of urban consolidation infrastructure providers should be encouraged to develop estimates of the long term cost of new investment, asset renewal and maintenance to guide strategic planning decisions about the balance between increasing the intensity of landuse in existing developed areas and extending into presently undeveloped areas.	decisions on the better use of existing infrastructure requires careful consideration of both capacity and appropriateness; essential that auditing be done on a site by site basis	for Melbourne and Sydney the proposed fringe developments are not viable and urban consolidation produces substantial net benefits Adelaide shows no particular benefit from urban consolidation urban consolidation in existing suburbs and more intensive forms of development on the fringe can provide significant savings in the provision of low cost housing

* not explicitly stated

The Dwyer Leslie report of 1991 for the New South Wales Department of Planning pointed out that only $11,300 of the Neilson estimate was for physical infrastructure. Dwyer Leslie estimated the potential savings at up to $30,700 of which between $7857 and $14,100 was estimated to fall in the public sector. But as has been pointed out elsewhere (Troy 1992b) even these latter estimates are highly sensitive to the assumptions of the study.

The National Housing Strategy report of 1991 estimated the development cost per allotment at $50,800 of which $22,500 was payable by the public sector. But this estimate included:

> Sewer, water, drainage, roads, power, telephone, site preparation, survey and design, and community facilities such as sports and recreational facilities, police, education, health, ambulance and fire stations (NHS 1991b: 66).

This report included the widest range of costs in the estimates but provided least information about their source.

In a paper in April 1992 Neilson and Spiller cited an EPAC (1991) study claiming that the capital cost "[T]o produce a new, fully serviced, lot on the urban fringe [was] somewhere between $50,000 and $70,000", although it provided no empirical evidence to justify the estimate. "Fully serviced" to them meant:

> [N]ot only the provision of on-site services (like water supply, sewers, power, made roads, local parks, and so on) but also pre schools, primary schools, secondary schools, hospitals, police stations, neighbourhood houses, various community facilities, regional and district parks, child care and public transport. (Neilson & Spiller 1992: 2)

Apart from wondering why they adopted such a limited list (they could have included power, telephones, postal services, council offices, courthouses, libraries, swimming pools, aged care centres—indeed, the whole range of services and facilities available in the city) the obvious point is that they imply that all these facilities are provided as and when each new lot has a house built on it. If this occurred there would be little need for public borrowing or for taxes or other revenue to pay interest on the costs of providing urban public investment. It is a very rare development in urban Australia for lots to be so provided with services or have access to facilities at the outset. Suburbs in the newest sector of Canberra, Gungahlin, for example had their pipe and wire services when the dwellings were completed but have had to wait years before schools and other social infrastructure was provided. Most services and facilities are provided in a lagged response to demand and many areas have been developed for many years, in some instances for generations of householders, before they enjoy such services. It is therefore misleading to imply that the full provision of the services and facilities occurs as lots are developed. An example may be found in the experience in New South Wales where councils seeking contributions under s 94 of *the Environmental Planning Assessment Act* 1979 (NSW) (EPAA) have required ever more complicated efforts to identify the nexus between proposed developments and the need for community facilities, their costs, their own program for the provision of the facilities and future cash flows. It is likely that many councils will discover sad miscalculations in their own cash flow situation which will leave them in financial difficulty and/or incapable of meeting the need for community facilities or the promises implicitly and explicitly made to new residents that the facilities would be provided.

In all the studies referred to above some of the services are services to property while others are provided on an area basis. A number of the services (eg energy and telephone) are commercially provided on a user pays basis and should not be included in the calculation. Community facilities such as sport and recreation facilities would be required wherever the population was located. These facilities are already under-provided in the inner areas and would be even more expensive to provide there than in new outer areas. Others, such as police, education, health and ambulance, should be regarded as rights of citizenship and not specific to particular development, and will vary little between areas if provided at uniform standards. Finally, fire stations are both a right of citizenship and largely financed by the private sector through insurance premiums, and are more expensive in higher density areas; they need more costly equipment and have higher turn out rates in higher density areas. This may reflect the higher degrees of risk and/or greater consequences of fire in such areas. It could also be argued that site preparation, survey and design are costs which will be incurred wherever the development occurs and may well be cheaper on new sites on the fringe because the problems they present are less complex and therefore easier to solve.

I Education Infrastructure

The issue of *spare capacity* in government schools deserves separate comment because it looms so large in calculations over alleged spare capacity in infrastructure in the inner areas and in the calculations for the cost of infrastructure provision on the fringe. It is also the only service for which a claim that it has surplus capacity could credibly be made. The notion of surplus capacity in schools is complex because it might relate to the capacity of school buildings to accommodate children, that is, to fixed capital costs, but it might also refer to the recurrent costs of teachers. We are not here concerned with the recurrent cost issues although that seems indirectly to be a significant element of the claims for economies made by proponents of consolidation.

The provision of schools, especially primary schools, was a central part of the postwar planning and development control system. Rapid population growth and urban development led to many schools being provided. The static planning models implicit in the development system of the early postwar period assumed that about 1000 households would be able to *sustain* a primary school. The catchment of the primary school became the building block of neighbourhood or community planning. One problem which emerged was that schools were rapidly provided in growth areas resulting in apparent surplus capacity once the population peak had passed, that is, once the *crop* of primary school aged children had passed through the schools. The aging of the population in any given suburb which had been rapidly developed to take advantage of economies in provision of network infrastructure services, especially water supply and sewerage, was thus accompanied by apparent massive surplus capacity in the schools. That is, the apparent over investment in schools came about in part because the government sought to make optimum use of other infrastructure services and did not take into account the longer term effects on the efficiency of the provision of schools. Reductions in family size in the subsequent generations meant that the schools would not reach their earlier planned capacity the second time around. Simultaneously, changes in education policy which led to higher proportions of school age children attending private schools, including transporting them out of areas where government schools had capacity to cope with them, exacerbated the apparent surplus capacity in government schools.

Changes in educational philosophy which more highly valued larger school units on the grounds that they offered more varied educational experiences coincided with increasing economism also exaggerated the apparent surplus capacity. To achieve the educational and administrative economic objectives schools were amalgamated or closed. Meanwhile continued population growth at the fringe led to demands for more schools. These demands coincided with the increasing financial difficulties facing State governments.

The *common sense* solution of seeking to minimise investment in schools by trying to focus that part of the population having children into areas where there were apparent surpluses in school capacity was powerfully attractive. Superficial analysis indicated that all that had to be done was to encourage the younger growing population into the inner areas. One problem was that in many of the inner areas, especially the older ones, the apparent surplus capacity was in schools which were no longer regarded as adequate for modern teaching, they were badly run down and they lacked recreation facilities now regarded as essential. Another was the comfortable assumption that simply forcing/encouraging people back to the areas in which the alleged surplus capacity existed would result in the same *crop* of children being accommodated in inner areas as was attracted to outer areas. Burnley (1983) has shown the fallacy of this demographic assumption. On average, the households who live in the higher density areas do not have as many children as those in lower density areas. Focusing redevelopment in an area because of the claimed surplus capacity in the schools may have the perverse effect of reducing the numbers of school children in that area.

To some extent the apparent surplus capacity in government schools arose because of the policy of using school buildings and facilities as single use facilities, that is, using them only for a limited range of educational activities. If the schools, especially primary schools, were used as accommodation for a range of educational, cultural and recreational activities and services, including child care services, the issue of over investment in educational infrastructure would be placed in perspective. For example, if the school and its provision was better planned in relation to the surrounding area and its rate of development, its construction could be phased so that its assembly halls, libraries and recreation facilities could be used for community uses. The alleged surplus capacity would thus be used for other desirable activities. Peak demands for school accommodation could have been (and often were) met by using transportable classrooms which could be moved to other sites once the peak had passed. Once the peak had passed it could also be apposite to adapt some part of the buildings and facilities for use as senior citizens' centres, continuing education centres and so on.

It is easier to understand how the alleged surplus capacity in the school system arose than to suggest what should be done about it. We have seen above how we might avoid the problem in the future by more flexibly planning for the peak demand for places and by making the schools serve multiple uses, possibly even converting some existing school accommodation to other community uses. Another response is to argue that it is premature to close schools or to change their use in the lower density middle and outer areas because changes in education lead to per capita increases in demand for space. In any event many such areas do *recover* their school age population, albeit to lower peaks, as turnover in population occurs and older generations die out to be replaced by younger generations in the child-bearing stages of household life. But redevelopment to higher density reduces the probability of this occurring.

The point is that it is misleading to raise investment in schools as a major public urban infrastructure investment issue in the same way as investment in services to property. Apart from the question of education investment being related to rights of citizenship it is clear that its costs and how they should be allocated are more affected by social policy rather than urban policy directed at the form of development. For this reason calculation of costs of investment in schools is not taken into account in this discussion of infrastructure costs.

When the proponents of consolidation do not understand the limitations of the figures they quote, it is small wonder that politicians, journalists and members of the public cannot make head nor tail of them. There are, of course, some commentators who do know or have had explained to them the limitations of the *costings* used but they persist in using them.

Issues of infrastructure costs are undoubtedly significant but we have yet to correctly identify them. Where the commentators do present data they tend to confine themselves to information produced by consultants' reports about the engineering costs of the provision of the service. Some reports also include a variety of services not normally classed as urban infrastructure which serves to confuse the debate. Most of the *studies* cited are commissioned consultancies embodying all the deficiencies such reports inherently contain. They tend to be designed as political documents to argue a case and do not impartially explore an issue. As a consequence the *facts* assembled are highly selected and can be used for another purpose only with great care.

One problem for people attempting to use the data is that they are usually estimates which rely heavily on the professional judgment of the author but the extent to which they do is not made clear so we cannot independently verify them. This is not a criticism of the authors of the reports but it is a reason for being cautious in using the data in them especially when they are so variable and so strongly contested. This is especially the case when we do not know the original purpose of the report.

The fact that the client commissioning the report holds the editorial control in a consultant report also tends to colour the findings.

The central assumption underlying consolidation policy that there is spare capacity in the infrastructure services including the water supply, sewerage, drainage and public transport system—especially the fixed rail train and tram systems—needs to be explored. Woodhead (1994: 45) points out that:

> The assumption that there is excess infrastructure capacity in inner city suburbs is frequently erroneous, the various hydraulic services in particular are rarely uniform in capacity and often require upgrading. The lack of knowledge as to the status of infrastructure is a matter of concern.

There is no doubt that in a general sense there is spare capacity in the fixed rail systems. But there is little spare capacity either in the track with present signalling systems or in the vehicles or platforms in the central parts of the network in peak periods. Increasing the demand for peak-period, centrally oriented public transport services without further investment of the kind undertaken for the Melbourne *loop* would more likely lead to a further reduction in the quality of the service because they would become even more overcrowded and delays would be longer leading to increased deficits in their operations, especially should governments succumb to pressures to invest in increased capacity.

The tantalising attraction is to try to increase the contra peak flow loadings on the systems by encouraging the development of employment at non-central locations on the network. This is a desirable objective and one cited in the plans for the metropolitan areas of most State capitals. But it requires a degree of control in employer location decisions which no one in government appears to be contemplating and for which none in the private sector have called. Because of the radial pattern of the existing rail service non-central locations are rarely served by more than one line. This fact alone should not automatically rule out encouraging contra peak flows as a policy option but in situations where property is in private ownership, planning control relies on passive, negative instruments and governments have themselves been remarkably averse to locating their own administrative departments out of the city centre and in such suburban nodes, the policy regrettably must have a low probability of success. In part the low level of success flows from the fact that the private sector has already re-centralised to a high degree in the development of new smaller scale suburban centres many of which are not on rail lines. Part of the attraction of the suburban centres lies in the fact that access to them is easier—by car. Nonetheless, a strong case can be made for encouraging State governments to pursue more vigorously an integrated regional centres policy, part of which would involve the development of the public transport system.

The comparisons between inner area redevelopment or consolidation and outer area lower density development usually understates the costs of the *disturbance*. The assumption that lower levels of capital costs are involved in consolidation because there is allegedly under-utilised capacity in the services is often in error because the costs of breaking into the existing services such as water supply and (especially) sewerage is frequently very high. The water supply and sewerage services in the older inner areas may have a significant economic life left if they are undisturbed but once they are broken into they tend to be expensive to connect and often break down as unforeseeable weaknesses emerge under the new loads. This often leads to earlier replacement or enhancement of the existing system. In addition the redevelopment to higher density in an area may well be restrained because there is a limit to the capacity elsewhere in the network.

Proposals for redevelopment or consolidation in Canberra provide two illustrations of this latter point: the proposed extension of the development of the suburb of Watson is constrained by the limited capacity in the sewer mains in the suburbs of O'Connor, Turner and Acton some distance away, the further redevelopment of the suburb of Kingston is similarly constrained by limitations in the capacity of the sewer main which serves the area. In both cases the original development for the suburbs did not anticipate the development now proposed and in both cases there is significant economic life in the existing sewers. Any reasonable comparison of the costs of development of these sites compared with development elsewhere must include the costs of early replacement and augmentation of the sewers. Proposals for redevelopment in Balmain in Sydney have raised similar issues.

The issue of infrastructure costs has been confused because the comparisons usually assume that the infrastructure provided to the fringe is new capital work and is so identified whereas the costs of *disturbance* in the inner older areas is often treated as maintenance of the existing system. As a result smaller developer charges are made for redevelopment. This difference in approach to accounting for the respective costs of consolidation versus fringe development can introduce significant distortions in the comparisons.

The argument that services were provided at standards which are too high may, in some locations, be accurate. But this *apparent over-provision* is often the result of prudent planning in the past. In the case of hydraulic services this is usually because the pipes were installed to allow subsequent expansion beyond a given area. Sometimes the *spare capacity* arises because of the requirement to install pipes of a specified minimum size. Inner city areas rarely have significant spare capacity. One of the ways local government authorities tried to cope with demands for roads in new areas during the 1960s and 1970s was to require developers to provide roads to a pavement thickness which was greater than the immediate needs of the estate. This arose in part because the local authorities were anticipating increased loads on the pavements which did not eventuate and in part because they were trying to minimise long-term maintenance costs. The subsequent changes in attitudes to drainage and the acceptability of *roll over* kerbing meant that road widths on residential estates could be reduced. By and large the modern standards of road provision in residential and industrial estates in particular cannot be regarded as excessive.

One of the areas where critics claim that standards are too high is in open space provision. Much of this criticism can be attributed to the general clamour for less regulation and is not related to any rigorous analysis. Suffice it to say that the provision of open space in the form of recreation facilities and parks is intimately connected with improvement of the environment and the health of the population and it is better to err on the side of caution than to reduce the standards. The general standard for Open Space in New South Wales is 2.83 hectares per 1000 population although some councils plan its provision to a higher standard. The temptation is always there for councils to succumb to pressures to reduce the standard of a particular development proposal because the population in an area has fallen.

There are two additional common assumptions which affect the estimates of savings in infrastructure arising from consolidation compared with outer area development:

- The population housed at the higher density in the inner area will travel to or from the CBD—that is they will find employment on the route of or convenient to the radially focused public transport system—and the bulk of their commercial and recreational interests will be able to be satisfied by using it. All the evidence we now have about the changing employment structure—especially as it affects job opportunities in the city centre—and the evidence about recreational and cultural activity patterns show this to be untrue. People living in the inner city travel, often by car, to a variety of destinations outside the inner city.
- The street and subdivision pattern of the lower density inner areas is appropriate for redevelopment to a higher density. Inner areas redevelopment puts more traffic on to parts of the road system that are already congested, unsafe and very costly to expand. Occasionally sites are amalgamated to allow for larger scale development but the circulation system is rarely reconsidered. The consequence is that instead of obtaining the alleged benefit of interesting new thoroughfares and pedestrian routes in an area, the piecemeal and generally small-scale and uncoordinated redevelopment which does occur is no improvement and

> frequently results in a lower level of amenity as the individual developers attempt to maximise development of their parcel of land. Kingston in Canberra provides an illustration of this point but there are many similar illustrations in Sydney and Melbourne. The manner in which redevelopment occurs limits the opportunity for savings in infrastructure provision and may well increase their costs. It may produce a lower level of amenity during the redevelopment phase as well as in its completed state.

A major problem with the comparisons of inner area higher density redevelopment versus traditional forms of development is that the comparisons are silent on the issue of relevant standards. The first and most obvious example is that the comparisons do not point out that, implicit in the *costings,* is a reduction in the provision of open space for passive and active recreation. They rarely point out that the schools in inner older areas are typically on small sites and built to older, lower standards and have less space for recreation activities than those in the newer, lower density areas. If the policy of consolidation produces the increase in population in the inner areas desired by its architects the residents of the areas will be required to accept lower standards of provision of open space and lower quality schools. Residents of the inner areas will also be required to accept higher accident rates because of the nature of the street layouts. The inner areas also generally have lower standards of urban services than are currently required.

An additional factor to be taken into account in any comparison of the relative costs of alternative policies is the opportunity to introduce new technology or new approaches to urban design. It is relatively easy to introduce new technology to new urban development and can be made a condition of any incremental growth. On the other hand it is often extremely difficult and costly to introduce or insert new technology for urban services when redeveloping existing areas. For example we can imagine how we can require new development to conform with natural drainage to minimise runoff, but it is well nigh impossible to do this in existing developed areas. It is similarly easy to see how new technology for water harvesting, supply, use and recycling could be progressively introduced at low cost in new areas but it would be very expensive to do so in the older existing areas.

Table 2.2

Actual (per lot) Costs of Provision of Infrastructure Services to a Selection of Typical Suburban Developments in Melbourne

	P1 1991	P1a 1994	P1b 1995	P2 1991	P2a nd	P3 1991	P3a 1992	P3b 1995	P4 1991	P4a 1994	P5 1989	P6 nd
Number of Lots	86	94	92	168	168	100	100	112	210	63	116	53
Area (ha)	5.9	7.5	6.6	12.4	12.4	11.0	11.0	10.3	16.7	5.8	9.3	3.0
Gross Residential Density (lot size – square metres)	688	792	716	736	736	1100	1100	920	795	916	803	566
Urban Services – Levies and Charges												
Sewer	1347	*	*	2094	2094	1431	1960	*	1385	1700	1160	1774
Water	570	*	*	1519	1519	47	500	*	434	1514	432	1547
Drainage	658	*	*	670	670	2487	2440	*	587	674		
Electricity	786	*	*	842	842	857	920	*	927	868	473	868
Total Levies and Charges	3361			5125	5126	4822	3360		3289	4756	2065	4189
Main Contract												
Road & Drain	*	*	*	*	*	*	7430	*	288	*	*	4811
Sewer Reticulation	*	*	*	*	*	*	2590	*		*	*	868
Water Reticulation	*	*	*	*	*	*	960	*		*	*	547
Contingency	*	*	*	*	*	*	500	*		*	*	189
Total Main Contact	8141	*	*	*	12,863	*	11,480	*	8328	6316	8090	6415
Supplementary Contract												
Landscaping/Fencing etc	*	*	*	*	*	*		*	587		*	*
Total Supplementary Contracts	*	*	*	*	*	*	2940	*	587	270	*	*
Total Main and Supplementary Contracts	8141	*	*	12,879	12,863	13,489	14,420	*	8915	6586	8090	6415

Development Costs												
Construction (incl charges)	*	21,569	*	*	*	*	*	*	*	*	*	*
Project Provision	3043	*	*	*	*	*	*	*	*	*	*	*
Reimbursements	*	*	*	*	*	*	-950	*	119	*	255	*
Apportioned Costs (+)	500	3503	3637	7590		2940	*	3205	2100	*	1[illegible]30	*
Apportioned Costs (-)	*	2686	*	2870		2940	*	*		3253	*	*
Engineering Fees	698	*	*	884	884	1416	1080	*	793	674	*	943
Survey Fees	344	*	*	278	277	311	410	*	414	451	1188	528
Council Supervision Fees	224	*	*	312	311	680	700	*	199	298	187	170
Landscape & Fencing	*	*	*	*	*	2800	2000	*	*	50	*	755
Rebates	*	*	*	*	*	156	1000	*	750	*	*	*
Other Misc	222	*	*	290	*	*	*	*	203	107	231	208
Total Development Costs	5031	*	*	6484	*	5363	4240	21,210	4578	4833	2783	2604
Total Development & Services Costs	16,533	22,386	25,469	24,491	24,415	24,173	24,480	24,415	16,949	16,175	12,928	13,509
Overheads												
Advertising	*	1300	1420	*	1000	*	1000	1620	*	*	*	1000
Agents Commission	*	1148		*	1113	*	751	*	*	*	*	814
Conveyancing/Titles	*	250	865	*	250	*	250	1120	*	113	*	250
Administration	*	3188	3075	*	3128	*	3225	3263	*	*	*	2321
Land Tax	*	723	*	*	214	*	160	*	*	*	*	660
Interest on Development	*	1544	*	2763	950	950	2763	*	*	*	*	1154
Total Overheads	6765	8153	5360	4925	6655	4925	8149	6003	4925	113	4900	6199
Total Development Costs (excl land costs)	23,298	30,539	30,829	29,416	31,070	29,098	32,629	30,418	21,874	16,469	17,828	19,708
Land	5111	*	5391	3655	3655	2473	2473	6886	1042	*	1896	2552
Interest	4477	*	*	1273	1273	1855	1855		1210	*	*	1590
Total Land Costs	9588	10,614	*	4928	4928	4328	4328	6886	2252	*	1896	4142
Grand Total All Costs	32,886	41,153	36,220	34,344	35,998	33,426	36,957	37,304	24,126	*	19,724	23,850

Note: * data not available or not applicable

New approaches to waste disposal, composting and mulching and at source waste separation and resource recovery may be practical responses which can be applied in both old and new traditional developments but cannot be contemplated in high density areas. These aspects are ignored in the present cost comparisons. We will return to this point in the next chapter.

The comparisons of costs focus on capital costs. They rarely include a full exploration of the recurrent costs, especially the costs to the environment, of the alternative forms of development. Some comparisons implicitly claim major savings in energy consumption from higher density development over the more traditional form of housing but they are rarely based on comparisons of system or whole of life energy consumption of the alternatives.

II Costs of Infrastructure Services

In this section we will examine the actual costs of provision of urban services to a selection of typical suburban developments in Melbourne. The projects are not chosen to present some statistically *defensible* analysis but they are chosen as typical of the kinds of urban developments which have recently occurred in that city. Similar cost comparisons are available for similar projects in Sydney and Adelaide.

The most obvious point which emerges from Table 2.2 is that infrastructure costs are significantly lower than Ministers or their advisers claim. The table shows that the full servicing costs for water supply, sewerage, drainage and roadworks on site ranges from $13,000 to $25,500. This long-lived infrastructure capital, although paid for by the dwelling owner at the time the service is provided is then vested in the service authority. That is, the costs of reticulation of the services are fully met privately at the beginning of their life so are not a call on public capital. Moreover, in most cases the costs include the costs of any trunk amplifications, especially of sewerage and drainage, made necessary by the development.

Each site contributed, to *headworks* for water supply, sewerage, drainage and roadworks from about $2100 to $5200 of which approximately $800 was for electricity undergrounding, which is also then vested in the relevant authority. These levies or contributions to headworks costs are a substantial and increasing part of those costs and again are *up front* charges which older sites in the metropolitan area were not required to bear. We should note too that these sites are required to pay the same annual charges for water supply and sewerage services as other areas, which means that the newer areas not only pay the capital costs of the services they receive but because of the way the charges are constructed they pay, through them, a component of the historic costs of providing the infrastructure to the older inner areas, including the cost of the loans raised to do so.

Even when we include the costs of overhead charges, including interest costs through the development stages, the costs of providing serviced land at densities close to traditional levels range from $17,800 to $32,400. Adding land costs and the interest on land holding increases the costs to between $19,700 and $41,200, which is significantly lower than the "$50,000 and 70,000" (excluding land and interest costs) claimed by Neilson and Spiller and other proponents of consolidation, and none of these costs are public sector costs. Not only do present development policies lead to full costs recovery of what were formerly regarded as public infrastructure services but those assets, privately funded, are handed over to the public sector and become parts of the public's assets. Sites on which redevelopment or dual occupancy developments occur are rarely required to contribute to infrastructure costs even when their connection to the systems result in significant upgrading.

A number of studies have now concluded that there are some savings to be gained from the provision of infrastructure services in higher density new developments compared with conventional forms of new housing although few now claim that the savings are as substantial as various State and Commonwealth Ministers have claimed. Fewer now claim significant savings from redevelopment projects. The higher costs of new higher density housing (assuming the same size and comparable quality of dwelling) compared with new conventional housing typically exceed the alleged infrastructure savings. The question must then be asked: where does the benefit lie in this outcome? We should also note that the higher density housing results in higher environmental stresses for its residents and on the ecological system generally and is less flexible than the traditional form of housing—points to which we return. It is also clear that many of the new *walk up* flats result in forbidding, unwelcoming environments — those near Liverpool in Sydney, sadly, being excellent examples of the poor quality development the policy has produced.

A high proportion of the new higher density housing is now occurring on the fringe of the city. This is a direct outcome of government policy and might be associated with lower physical infrastructure costs compared with redevelopment of inner areas, but it produces the perverse *doughnut* effect of an annulus of high density housing ringing the lower density middle suburbs. The greater accessibility claimed for inner suburban consolidation does not occur. Much of the housing in the higher density areas has lower provision of services, particularly schools and open space. In Sydney until 1993 local authorities could not levy dual occupancy developments for contributions under s 94 of the EPAA for the provision of community facilities and open space. Although councils were given that power in 1993 provided they could establish a nexus between the proposed development and the demand for services and they had adopted a Control Plan for the area the effect of dual occupancy development has been to reduce the standard of provision of community facilities and services. There is a strong probability that these locations will become stigmatised and be seen as less desirable.

III Physical and Social Infrastructure

Infrastructure services can be divided into two categories. Most discussion is focussed on the network or *pipe and wire* services of physical infrastructure meaning the roads, the water, sewerage, drainage and gas pipe networks and the lacework of power and telephone lines of the city which connect properties to one another. The waste disposal system is also often grouped under this heading even though it is not a network in the sense of fixed capital. We may conveniently regard it as a service to property.

Social infrastructure, on the other hand, provides the area-based services such as schools, hospitals and health centres, libraries, community facilities, recreational space, police and fire services. Each of them typically implies a commitment to the provision of fixed capital in the form of buildings but their recurrent costs are a function of the demand, which varies with population.

Neutze (1994) suggests that we should approach the financing of these services in different ways and for some of them we should completely re-think the basis on which they are provided. He argues that we should not rely on developer contributions to the extent we do and that we should make greater use of location specific user charges. These would lead to charges related to the cost of coping with water demand, drainage, sewerage, sewage treatment and with congestion or peak pricing for transport services. The method of charging for waste collection and processing could also be structured to allow for volume and complexity of the waste stream. The calculation of user charges should also allow the inclusion of resource rents for water and air quality.

We should ask whether we can find a better, cheaper more modern way of providing the infrastructure services with less environmental stress. Can we reshape or moderate the demand for the services? How should we provide and price the services? Would changes in pricing produce changes in demand for the services? We will discuss these questions in Chapter 3.

A major problem with most of the discussion about housing and related urban issues and the policy positions which have been adopted is that little consideration appears to have been given to the problems of transition. Most of the discussion and policy is ahistorical, indicating little understanding of the economic and social processes which led to the present situation or of their influence on the course of development, especially in the short term; it implicitly refers to some *desirable* physical end state without acknowledging that much of the analysis is highly contested, that the *desirable* end state is built on assumptions about urban life-styles which are highly elitist while ignoring the length of time, difficulties and dislocations involved in reaching it. We shall return to this point later when we explore alternative ways of delivering urban services.

A number of studies have been influential in the debate over the alleged *sprawl* of the Australian city. Many of the studies have been of urban development elsewhere. Students of public policy are acutely aware of the problems and limitations of cross-cultural or international comparisons. They usually go to some length to qualify or interpret any conclusion they might reach or recommendation they might make for Australian policy arising from such studies. For reasons that are not clear debates over urban policy which rely on international comparison seem to have ignored this simple but critically important point. Proponents of high urban density in Australia argue as though there are immutable laws governing the form and structure of cities which are little affected by the social and political aspirations of the people or the economic circumstances in which they find themselves.

An American study *The Cost of Sprawl* (Council on Environmental Quality 1975) has been used to justify the present consolidation policy in Australia. Those who cite it in Australia seldom acknowledge the political context and purpose or the methodological limitations of the study. In reviewing the study, Americans, Altshuler and Gomez-Ibanez (1993: 69) point out that the term *sprawl* itself is imprecise and that "[F]inding meaning in the cost differences is difficult because the quality of the housing units in the different communities is not comparable." They conclude that:

> Redevelopment and development on vacant land, then, have strikingly different implications about increasing development densities. Each increment of density and infrastructure capacity usually will be more expensive then the last if development involves the rebuilding or infilling of existing communities to higher densities. While higher density may provide modest infrastructure savings over low density when development occurs on vacant land, higher density may also cause disproportionate increases in infrastructure costs if the development occurs within existing built up areas . . . land development tends to be a less important cause of rising infrastructure demand than other forces, such as rising incomes or stricter standards for infrastructure services. Variations in urban form (such as *sprawl* or jobs–housing imbalance), moreover, appears to have modest effects on infrastructure costs. (Altshuler & Gomez-Ibanez 1993: 76)

Neilson and Spiller (1992) and Spiller (1992) imply that estimated savings of 44 per cent which the report claims for American situations of high density over lower density developments can be made in the provision of infrastructure to higher density housing compared with traditional density development in Australia. They do not point out the cultural/political context of the American study, the different ways in which infrastructure is provided in America or discuss why they believe the study's conclusions apply to Australia. The paper by Neilson and Spiller does, however, show that the comparison with

Australia is inappropriate. The definition of *sprawl* cited by them from the American study simply does not apply in Australia because development control and the way infrastructure is provided eliminated that form of development in Australia early in the postwar period. This basic flaw raises doubts over their argument that more compact forms require less capital investment in aggregate and that they are less demanding in terms of recurrent costs.

But in any case most of the costs, or many of them, are paid by developers in Australia and are passed on to the buyers. Some developers find it profitable to develop at higher density currently because they are not required to pay for services which exist. In effect they sell sites with services which have been funded by earlier owners. This is most obvious in Sydney where Councils have difficulty extracting EPAA s 94 contributions for dual occupancy developments. The only deterrence which developers recognise is over supply in the market which makes it difficult for developers to sell their projects. Unfortunately the over supply has to occur before developers recognise it. Developers are not sophisticated in their analysis of supply or demand or the factors which affect them.

But the most devastating unintentional critique of present policy and the claims made that traditional forms of development are too costly is provided by a report published by the Australian Urban and Regional Development Review entitled *Smart Planning Not Sprawl* (AURDR 1995). The report purports to make the case for planning compared with urban *sprawl*. In this it sets up a *straw man* argument because the kind of planning whose virtues it sings has been practised in most States since the early 1950s, although it is relatively novel in Queensland. The report begins by summarising several studies that estimated costs of infrastructure and how the costs varied with lot size. The first point to note is that the costs are significantly lower than any of the *cost* figures used by Commonwealth Ministers such as Howe, formerly Minister for Housing and Regional Development. The second is that the report compares costs for different forms of new development in southeastern Queensland, an area which has hitherto had low levels of planning control, and finds that increasing the net residential density by 50 per cent (from 10 to 15 dwellings per hectare) results in a saving of 3 per cent (AURDR 1995: 15). A *saving* which depends on more planning and an *interconnective* layout (which would generate more road accidents and which is insensitive to the site topography) and would be less if the full range of costs, for example those for drainage and waste disposal, were taken into account. The third point is that cost effective sequencing of development results in significant savings at all densities and that most of these savings are in the provision of social infrastructure, especially schools.

We could take issue with many of the assumptions and arguments made in the report and they would only serve to further reduce the difference between the example of development at 10 dwellings to the hectare compared with those at higher densities. We note too that the report is silent on the cost comparisons between traditional development of new areas and redevelopment of older areas.

The conclusion we reach is that the claim made for significant infrastructure cost savings by developing cities to higher density is overstated. Where such savings do accrue in infrastructure costs they may be offset by increased costs of construction at the higher density or increased recurrent costs of urban services. They will also be accompanied by loss of amenity. The question which has to be posed is: if the infrastructure savings are as small as the report identifies but people are prepared to pay them why should policy be directed to forcing people to live at higher density?

Chapter 3

THE ENVIRONMENTAL IMPERATIVE

A major justification for the consolidation policy is that it will be beneficial to the environment. Environmental issues are clearly of major concern. Problems of air, water and noise pollution manifest themselves mainly in the major urban centres. It is also clear that the way we live in and pursue our activities in cities creates the problems of concentration of wastes we describe as pollution. Although there is agreement that environmental considerations embrace a range of critical issues, only one has been given great weight in exploring current housing and urban policy. In focusing on one aspect of energy consumption the present consolidation policy emphasises only one of the sources of environmental stress. The effect of energy consumption on the creation of the greenhouse effect is undoubtedly important (Troy 1990). The problem is that in the debate over housing and urban policy the focus on energy consumption and its implication for air pollution and the greenhouse effect has largely been reduced to a consideration of the energy consumed in the transport system. The dominance of a *scientific environmentalism* has led to the claim that changing the form of the city by increasing its density will reduce transport energy consumption which will thus reduce air pollution and the greenhouse effect. The fact that much of the scientific evidence for the greenhouse effect is contested or that the natural system has a greater capacity to cope with greenhouse gases, particularly CO_2, than was hitherto understood is ignored in the struggle for influence over policy priorities. Another feature of consolidation policy is that it is founded on a conception of end state planning which takes no account of the length or problems of transition or the opportunities which might develop in that period.

I An Alternative Approach

Much of the debate about housing and urban policy has been couched within a dominant paradigm about the nature of the Australian city which has ignored what has been happening in them and the influence of their history on their futures. It has been a debate built on crude physical determinism and static relationships especially those which are claimed to exist between transport and land use and a structure which no longer reflects the disposition of activities or aspirations of the city's residents. But let us return to the beginning.

We should be careful to avoid explanations of what has been happening in terms which are overly technologically deterministic. It is clear, however, that a number of technological innovations in the postwar period have been taken up or exploited in a fashion that has resulted in major restructuring forces which have changed the nature of many activities carried out in the cities, and rearranged their spatial relationships. For example changes in marine transport have led to a sequence of changes in harbours, their location in the metropolitan area and their relationship to the city centre and to industry.

The progressive redevelopments of the major wharves in Sydney, which were occasioned by progress—from wooden hulled ships to mild steel; from sail power through reciprocating steam engines to steam turbines and diesel power; from a few hundred to thousands then tens of thousands of tons; from general cargo to bulk and container shipping—all wrought major changes in the storage and handling of cargo and thus the operation of *port side* activities. These changes have also been accompanied by increasing reliability in equipment and improved navigational aids. Ships now travel faster and in spite of their increase in size turn around faster. They are managed and maintained in different ways and have different and much smaller crews. Each change has affected the relationship of the port to the city.

Whereas once the Sydney CBD was actually in the middle of all the marine transport activity and was alive with seamen, waterside workers and those who serviced the ships, the bulk of these activities are now carried out 12 kilometres from the centre so the people and colour they brought have gone. A similar story can be told for all the major port cities in Australia (and elsewhere, for that matter).

Retailing technology has also changed and with it the relationship between retailers and their suppliers as well as their customers, resulting in further massive changes in the city. The growth of the supermarket, changes in the retailing of fruit, vegetables and meat has been attended by the development and wide availability of household refrigerators and freezers which has led to once-a-week shopping thereby reducing the reliance on local stores. The more recent extension of shopping hours and the development of very large supermarkets have even further reduced the reliance on local stores.

Changes in manufacturing processes and materials handling have led to changes in factory layouts and locations. Simultaneously changes in labour deployment and management have led to significant changes in the use of people and their movement to and from factories. Warehousing and distribution has changed due to different methods of materials handling, stock and inventory control. Innovations in control technology have wrought changes in organisational structures. Developments in information technology have led to changes in information collection, transmission and processing which have in turn been reflected in major changes in the office and executive functions in firms and government agencies. This technology has also led to changes in cultural and recreational activities.

The development of the motor vehicle has led to cheaper, more reliable, more flexible and, eventually, less polluting transport. Moreover, the attractions of motor vehicles have been seen as a way of giving effect to or expressing the dominant values of freedom of choice and the emphasis on individualism in Australian society. Over the same period living standards have risen, increasing independence and leisure time.

This list of changes is not exhaustive but it serves to make the point that the urban system has been subjected to a variety of dynamic processes and has responded accordingly. Some of these technological innovations, changes in labour management and working and trading practices have been adopted rapidly and have quickly influenced the structure of the city. Few of them were foreseen. The response has, however, reshaped and been shaped by both the inherited physical plant and the inherited political and institutional structures of the city.

One of the lessons we can draw from this understanding is that we must recognise that there will be further innovations which will flow from the needs of domestic, commercial and industrial imperatives and we can ensure that, in adopting them, they have beneficial impacts including resolution of problems of environmental stress currently experienced in the city. In this lie the clues as to how we might fashion an alternative approach to housing and urban policy.

We turn now to discuss how we might incorporate concerns for the environment in fashioning housing and urban policy.

II Ecologically Sustainable Development

The notion of sustainable development or *ecologically sustainable development* (ESD), to use the fuller term, has been coined to make the point that we should pursue development only so long as it is in balance with the environment. It has become a popular rallying cry but what does it mean in relation to our cities? In the reports recently commissioned by the Federal Government into ESD (Ecologically Sustainable Development Working Group Reports, 1991a– 1991i) the *city* was not used as a unit of analysis or way of approaching the problems and hardly rated a mention except indirectly through a partial examination of transport issues.

What does ESD mean? In contemporary debates it is defined in several ways: The following is a brief selection of definitions from a range of sources.

"Sustainable development is development that meets the needs of the present without compromising the ability of future generations to meet their own needs." (World Commission on Environment and Development 1987: 43.)

The "Concept of Ecologically Sustainable Development . . . essentially is about changing the way we approach and manage human progress and ensure the prosperity of future generations." (Department of Primary Industries and Energy, 1991b: 7.)

While there is no universally accepted definition of ESD, in 1990 the Commonwealth Government in an ESD strategy discussion paper suggested the following definition for ESD in Australia: "Using, conserving and enhancing the community's resources so that ecological processes, on which life depends, are maintained, and the total quality of life, now and in the future, can be increased." (Department of Prime Minister & Cabinet 1990 cited in Ecologically Sustainable Development Steering Committee 1992: 6.)

"The Australian Government added the word ecologically" to the term sustainable development—the only government in the world that has modified the concept outlined in *Our Common Future*. (ESD newsbrief, Issue No 2, July 1991: 8.)

Although the term embodies a commitment to equity, at least in the sense of intergenerational equity, environmentalists, developers and politicians all use the term but it is clear that it has different meanings for speaker and listener, writer and reader, which alone should alert us to a major problem. Any term which can mean whatever the speaker/writer or listener/reader wants it to mean provides little guidance or discipline in policy formulation or program administration. The recent focus on environmental issues and concerns is to be welcomed. But real problems emerge when we attempt to translate those concerns into the formulation of housing and urban policies and programs.

Modern cities are inherently ecologically unsustainable because they need to import food, energy and raw materials and they produce more waste than they can cope with within their boundaries and because they radically change the ecology of their sites. Moreover, the larger the concentration of population, that is, the bigger the city, the more unsustainable it is. Even if we extend the boundary of the city to include its hinterland we cannot usefully describe it as potentially ecologically sustainable. The more the city becomes part of the international economic order the less it can be seen as *ecologically sustainable* in any operational sense. To hold out such a beguiling but unattainable prospect is ultimately to diminish the legitimate concerns for the environment because it leads people to the view that nothing can be done to overcome or alleviate the problem.

The only urban strategy which seems environmentally sensible is one which has as its goal the minimisation of environmental stress within and outside the city. Some services may be able to be provided without placing any stress on the environment whereas for others, using present technology and with present social behaviour, this may be too expensive. Acceptance of an obligation to reduce environmental stress in the development of the city is acceptance of the need for more planning and control. Paul Ashton characterised Sydney as an "[A]ccidental" city. That is, he charts its development as a series of unplanned initiatives which only accidentally resulted in some good design, some good quality urban spaces (Ashton 1993). To achieve a systematic and sustainable reduction in environmental stress in the future the city will need to be developed according to some plan—it will need to become an intentional city, it will need to be good by design!

In applying the concept of minimisation of environmental stress to the development and management of urban areas and in particular to housing policy we should think about it in two ways:

- how it should apply to existing development and
- how it should apply to new development.

In the following section we consider a series of services and environmental issues. In selecting the service for discussion we focus first on those we might consider *basic* to human life. That is, we first consider the water cycle, food production, waste generation, air pollution, energy consumption and finally the derived demands of transport and communication.

III Water Capture, Water Consumption, Recycling, Drainage and Sewerage

The environmental stress resulting from the way we have exploited water for rural activities and the effect on water supply and quality of land clearing and farming practices is a major concern but this discussion focuses on the environmental stress in the water system due to the development and operation of urban areas. We explore the issue of water capture, water consumption, recycling, drainage and sewerage at some length here because it is claimed that consolidation will reduce the demand for capital for these services and will reduce the environmental stresses resulting from their use.

1 Established areas

In this driest of continents we have structured the water supply agencies and used a supply technology and method of funding consumption in a manner which has discouraged the harvesting of water which falls on the urban areas as rain. Furthermore, the pricing policies pursued have not encouraged economy in the use of water supplied (Dingle & Rasmussen 1991; Lloyd, Troy & Schreiner 1992).

Since the late nineteenth century Australian cities have organised their supplies of potable water by impounding nearby rivers and reticulating the water throughout the city. The water has usually required little treatment and has been of very high quality. It has been used once and then discharged, mostly via the sewerage system to the ocean and the remainder via the drainage system to creeks and rivers. In many cases the catchment areas of the rivers which have been harvested have been open to only limited uses to avoid pollution of the water supply. The policy has had a number of disadvantages including progressive disruption of the eco-systems of the rivers whose waters have been impounded. The high variability in rainfall, the likelihood of periodic droughts and the political sensitivity of water shortages has led urban water authorities to build dams and water storages capable of holding enough water to sustain urban areas for long periods.

The growth of the major cities and the increase in per capita consumption of water has reached the point where we now face a crisis in our capacity to meet the demand. The attempt to meet the demand for additional supplies under the prevailing system of *once only use* is now being challenged due to the increasing cost of harvesting waters at increasing distances from the cities and due to the increasing concern for the environment. We should note, however, that early evidence of the effect of the new water pricing policies is that water consumption is now falling.

The profligate attitude to water consumption has had the immediate effect of creating a serious problem of drainage in urban areas. Until recently the pricing policies followed by the water authorities did not encourage individuals or firms either to be economical in the use of water or to harvest the water which falls on their property as rain. As development has occurred the proportion of the urban area covered with pavement and hard standing has increased. This has increased the runoff from those areas and, in particular, has increased the peakedness of the runoff because the runoff from hard surfaces is virtually instantaneous—there is little retention or delay. Contemporary gardening practices have also served to increase the runoff of rainfall. The net effect of these practices has been to create a *drainage problem* which increases volume and intensity with density of development to reach a maximum when the area is fully covered by impervious materials or surfaces.

The volume of water now draining off not only causes acute local flooding, especially in areas which have undergone or are undergoing redevelopment, it also causes massive pollution in the receiving water ways because of the material transported by the surface water. This material includes oils, rubber and brake lining dust from motor cars, animal droppings, insecticides, weedicides, garden fertilisers, rubbish including bottles, cans and take-away food containers, silt and vegetable detritus. Much of this material results in heavy local loads on the environment and the silt, vegetable detritus, bottles, cans and food containers often accumulate resulting in loss of amenity and danger for those using recreational facilities affected by the runoff. The pollution load of storm water runoff can lead to massive deterioration as occurs increasingly in the Hawkesbury River in Sydney. The solid material transported by the stormwater may also cause drainage pipes to be blocked which then causes local flooding, which may be extremely costly in terms of damage to property. One benefit of the stormwater runoff is that it does periodically *clean* the roads and so on albeit at the cost of pollution of the creeks and rivers. The pollution load could be reduced by construction of interceptors and stilling basins in the drainage line. Residents should also be educated to use less weedicide, insecticide and fertiliser in gardens from which water is shed. Any policy which reduced the runoff would have to be accompanied by policies to reduce the build up of waste material on roads and parking areas and so on.

Until recently, regulations discouraging the use of rainwater storage tanks to store roof runoff exacerbated the problem. The *drainage problem* has been made more serious because of the institutional manner in which the problem has been addressed. In most cities drainage has been seen as a local problem: the responsibility of the local government authority with few effective measures being taken to treat the problem as a metropolitan wide issue. Although it might seem to be a good idea to solve the problem close to where it originates, the consequence is that developers and owners of the higher land have solved *their* problem by ensuring that their parcels of land were well drained but with little concern for those lower down the drainage basin. The policy has encouraged individuals to cope with drainage from their parcel of land in a sort of *bugger thy neighbour* approach which has frequently resulted in those lower down the catchment having to cope with flooding. This has included local authorities being content to ensure that they *got their drainage away* even at the cost of down stream authorities. The limited resources available to local authorities has meant that they have been unable to take appropriate measures to resolve the issues.

It is increasingly evident that the environmental stresses caused by the way sewage is discharged to the ecosystem is unacceptably high. Sewage from residential areas is relatively benign but when it is mixed with water-borne wastes from industry and commerce a waste stream is produced that can be difficult to process. The volume of sewage produced can also create a problem when the treated effluent is discharged to rivers or the ocean. When the sewage flow is high relative to river flows it can easily exceed the capacity of the river's natural system to *process* the waste. Eutrophication may occur as a result of which the river may become a health hazard. The sheer volume of sewage produced in large cities and discharged to the ocean through a small number of outfalls may also lead to such high point discharges of pollutants that the local capacity of the ocean to receive the wastes is exceeded and leads to local destruction of the ecosystem. The high volumes discharged may also lead to wastes being washed up on local beaches destroying their amenity and presenting local health hazards.

The way we supply and price water in urban areas has also led to increased environmental stress in the catchment of rivers, the waters of which have been impounded to provide the assured supply for the operation of the urban areas, because we have often affected their ecological balance.

There seems to be a *prima facie* case for concluding that the way water is used in urban areas is unsustainable. At one end of the system the harvesting and storage of water leads to major environmental disruption and at the other we create massive point sources of pollution as we concentrate the sewage and discharge it to the ocean. A more appropriate approach would be to develop an integrated water system which viewed the supply of water at various levels of quality and the waste water system as one system instead of the two different systems we currently have. Such a system would also enable storm water runoff to be treated as part of the same system.

There can be little doubt historically that the centralised control over water supply enabled its quality to be assured. The resulting great improvements in health and the reduction in diseases such as cholera implicitly empowered the institutions created to store and deliver potable water and to receive and discharge sewage (and ultimately, in many jurisdictions, to provide a drainage system) to continue much as they have. A consequence is that we have maintained a nineteenth century approach to the delivery of hydraulic services with little change in the fundamental technology. We should note here that the engineering of new dams, pipe installations and treatment plants has frequently been innovative and the introduction of telemetry and information technology to system control has been highly advanced, but the reliance on large-scale networks has rarely been queried. We have persisted with *big* engineering solutions and highly hierarchic organisations. Consequently, the system impact of the way water is harvested, stored, supplied and used has rarely been re-examined.

In looking at the consumption of water we must explore ways of moderating behaviour of present residential, industrial, and commercial consumers. In doing so it is important to recognise the different demands for water from those different consumers and, in particular, the different streams of waste-as-sewage they produce.

Behaviour may be moderated by educational and information programs, regulatory regimes and by better use of pricing mechanisms. Various water authorities have embarked on programs to educate consumers to better water usage practices. For residential consumers these have included advice on the use of lower phosphate detergents, most efficient ways and times for garden watering which currently accounts for about one-quarter of water used (about one-half the summer consumption), the amount of water wasted by a dripping tap, encouraging the use of dual flush toilet cisterns, reuse of washing suds and the benefits of *shower miser* installations. In some water authorities this advice has been accompanied by the introduction of water pricing policies which place a greater burden on those who use the most water. This mixed strategy has been very effective in the Hunter Valley, where domestic water consumption has fallen dramatically, and in Sydney, where domestic consumption has also fallen.

Table 3.1

Average Annual Water Consumption and Rainfall

	Domestic Water Consumption[a] (kl)	Rainfall[b] mm	Potential Water Capture from a 150m² Roof (kl)	% of Water Consumption
Median				
Melbourne	270	653	98	36.3
Sydney	265	1160	174	65.7
Canberra	402	630	95	23.6
Brisbane	437	1107	166	38.0
Lowest year				
Melbourne	270	332	50	18.5
Sydney	265	583	87	32.8
Canberra	402	261	39	9.7
Brisbane	437	576	86	19.7
Highest year				
Melbourne	270	874	131	48.5
Sydney	265	2194	329	124.2
Canberra	402	1162	174	43.3
Brisbane	437	2170	326	74.6

Sources: Water consumption – *Pricing Systems for Major Water Authorities in Australia*, ARMCANZ Water Forum, Financial and Corporate Management Committee, Ed 3 April 1993 and Ed 4 May 1994; Rainfall – Bureau of Meterology, Canberra.

Note: (a) Average of years 1991/1992, 1992/1993 & 1993/1994; (b) high/low rainfall figures are for Sydney Bureau of Meterology Office, Melbourne Regional Office, Canberra Airport, Brisbane.

The relatively recent removal of regulations (originally introduced to provide financial security for the water authorities and later justified on health grounds) prohibiting the use of domestic rainwater tanks in urban areas together with the introduction of appropriate pricing for water consumption should result in greater numbers of households capturing roof runoff for use in garden watering and other domestic uses. This will reduce demand for *scheme* water and simultaneously reduce or attenuate runoff and therefore drainage.

Educational programs have limited value with industrial and commercial consumers. For this group a combination of enforcement of regulations and pricing signals are more effective. Pricing water and sewage appropriately has led to a dramatic reduction in water consumption for industry and commerce. Here again the experience in the Hunter Valley has been most efficacious. Water recycling has increased and industrial processes redesigned with the result that the amount of water used in steel making for example has fallen from 26 to 2.8 tonnes of potable water per tonne of liquid steel and with new processes being introduced is expected to fall to 2.2 (D Audet and A Yarovy, pers comm August 1995). Sydney Water has introduced effluent pricing policies which have encouraged firms to redesign processes which have led to the reduction both in the volume and complexity of their wastes.

Opportunities exist or can be created to reshape the way we consume or recycle water because older parts of the system need to be replaced. Indeed, some older parts of some of the systems are now failing in spectacular fashion, eg in Melbourne (the *Age* 1992, 28 November: 3, 6 December: 16; 1993, 8 January: 8, 24 January: 1, 25 January: 5, 26 January: 3; 1 February: 6).

But there is another way of looking at the *problem.* Table 3.1 sets out the rainfall and average water consumption in selected cities. The rain falling on the average roof (house and garage) area of 150 square metres in those cities is potentially able to meet as much as 10 per cent of the demand for water consumption in Canberra and 18 per cent in Melbourne in the most serious drought conditions. It is potentially enough to meet a quarter of the present demand for Canberra, over one third for Melbourne and Brisbane and over two-thirds for Sydney more than half the time. In the wetter years the rainfall alone exceeds the amount used in garden watering. The point of these simple illustrative calculations is to show that even with a *once only* use as garden water, harvested rainfall could meet a high proportion of the demand for garden watering which accounts, on average, for one-quarter of household consumption. If grey water (shower, bath and washing water) was collected as a part of an integrated system for use as recycled water to flush toilets (and, if treated to an appropriate level, for showers and washing and so on) and water gardens in addition to the rainfall, the water would exceed the demand for garden water even in extreme drought years in all cities. Canberra and Brisbane have household water consumption levels about 50 per cent higher than Sydney and Melbourne. The introduction of water pricing and an education program devised to encourage households to make better use of water may well reduce these consumption levels in which case the rainfall could potentially meet a higher proportion of the demand from households in those cities. The precise level of *savings* available in the demand for reticulated water and in terms of reduced runoff would depend on the actual roof area, the proportion of rainfall *harvested*, the storage capacity of the necessary tanks, the variability of rainfall throughout the year and the seasonal consumption of water, especially for garden watering. The volume of savings would also be affected by the price of reticulated water, the cost of collecting and storing water from the roof and the cost of the recycling system for grey water. At present the costs of water supplied by the central water authorities is lower than those of private water harvesting by use of tanks, and so on. But these relativities would change if the costs of storm water runoff were taken into account and if a resource rent was charged for the water harvested by the water authorities from the rivers and streams whose flows they intercept.

The strategy to be adopted in existing parts of urban areas should be shaped according to whether it is feasible to redesign the existing systems for water distribution, sewerage and drainage. In the first phase of *conversion* of traditional residential areas where there are few industrial and commercial consumers in many cases it should be possible to encourage residents to install tanks to store rain water for domestic consumption. In a second phase it may prove feasible to identify developed areas in which the sewerage system could be redeveloped to encourage the use of local treatment plants using new technologies (membrane technology being one possibility) in such a way that the treated effluent could be recycled for use in the same area. This would result in the development of a dual system water supply and drainage system. Because of the way water is supplied under gravity flow this could be conceived of as a *cascade system* with the recycled water, depending on its quality and whether it met appropriate health standards, being available for domestic use or for public uses such as park and garden watering (a new system of *mining* water from sewers in the Australian Capital Territory shows how this can be integrated with the present sewerage system (*Better Cities* 1995)), aquifer recharging, creation of recreation facilities, irrigation or for aquaculture including fish farming for areas progressively lower down the drainage gradient. To what extent any of these uses can be employed depends on the open space system, the topography of the site, the type of soil and the basic geological structures in an area. Clearly, the system would continue to need some central storage capacity to fight fires and to provide back-up storage but it would not need to have as large a capacity and it would interfere less with the river ecology and reduce the problem of large-scale effluent flows.

In those residential areas where it is appropriate, the policy response should be also to encourage people to compost their kitchen and garden wastes and to use the resulting mulch in their gardens. The benefit of this would be that water consumption for gardening would be reduced because the tilth of the soils would be improved thus increasing the capacity of the soils to absorb rainfall and reducing runoff and therefore drainage. An additional benefit in composting would be a reduction in the demand for landfill waste disposal sites and a reduction in the cost of garbage collection.

2 New development

Residential

The hydrological characteristics of catchments are changed by development. The result has been that in many areas which have been developed from rural use, or even *bushland*, peak runoffs have resulted in local flooding in the resulting urban area. Later redevelopment of those areas to higher density usually changes the characteristics again, resulting in a higher intensity of flooding until expensive remedial work is undertaken. One way around this problem is to adopt the principle of natural drainage design in which development is designed to accord well with the catchment and not the pattern of land ownership. Under this principle the objective is to minimise runoff by facilitating soakage and to attenuate the peaks of that water which must unavoidably drain away. Capturing and harvesting the rainfall by storing it on site also serves this purpose. New housing can be constructed to harvest rain water for domestic uses, providing that health standards are not compromised, and to make better use of recycled water for toilet flushing, garden watering, and so on. The gardens and dwellings are then designed to reduce water consumption. This may involve a dual system of local recycling of grey water for use in toilet flushing and garden watering. It could also involve toilet systems which separated urine flows from faeces with the urine flows being composted for fertiliser and with the faeces and other domestic waste water being diverted through sludge traps with the resulting sludge being composted and the effluent being *treated* to be used in garden watering and so on.

The new approach to design also requires a new approach to paving and hard standing. Roads, footpaths and hard standing should be designed to be less impervious so that they shed less of the water which falls on them or shed it in such a way that it is directed into public and private gardens and ponds and its runoff is slowed.

The design of large residential estates or areas should be directed to increasing the retention of rainfall for the maintenance of public open space including playing fields which may also be designed to retard the runoff to reduce drainage. It will be possible to undertake modifications to the drainage systems in some existing residential areas to achieve these ends. We could establish a development condition requiring developers to take measures to ensure that the runoff was no higher than prior to development. This would encourage the harvest of rainfall for use in the gardens or for domestic uses.

In some areas locally ponded runoff can be used as a recreational facility and, with proper management, the ponds and reservoirs can be used for aquaculture including the production of fish for food.

Industry/commerce

Where possible the rainfall should be harvested (such as capturing roof water) but in most cases this will be less practical than in residential development. Greater attention should be paid to the industrial and commercial processes using water and, with appropriate pricing policies, in these circumstances more of the water used would be recycled. Simultaneously, greater attention should be given to effluent quality control which would encourage at-source separation and recovery of *wastes* which in turn would reduce the volume and complexity of the sewage in the public mains.

The improvement of sewage treatment and increased possibility for recycling in both existing and new areas might also depend to a significant degree on the adoption of an appropriate regulatory regime. Even allowing for better use of pricing strategies it may prove to be necessary to strictly regulate the use or discharge of particular products or chemicals because even small amounts of them are inimical to the operation of waste treatment processes or have demonstrated and/or possible long-term deleterious effects on the ecological system. Whether recycling is feasible will depend on factors such as soil conditions and whether the scheme is large enough to economically provide the competent technical oversight of the necessary treatment plants.

This discussion suggests that the demand for the services can be reshaped in ways which reduce environmental stress without necessarily changing the form of the city: consolidation will not necessarily reduce the demand for services and, in the form being pursued, will increase environmental stress.

The major benefit of the alternative approach outlined above for existing and future development would flow both from the reduced need for large-scale investment in dams, trunk mains and pumping systems and from a reduction in the load on the existing systems. This latter point has particular significance in the sewerage systems because the systems now in place in the older inner areas of the cities are nearing the end of their operational lives. The mains had a design life of 100 years which is now being reached. The water authorities have, in many cases, developed techniques to reline and refurbish mains thus extending their lives for a time, but in many instances they will have to be replaced. Doing so in an operating city is complex and expensive. The introduction of systems of coping with waste streams by reducing the volume of their flow and by reducing the centralisation of the flows not only enables the cheaper replacement of the old pipe networks and treatment plants, it also has the potential to reduce the pollution problem by reducing the concentration at the outfalls to the ocean. Although there is implicit recognition in this argument of the need to change or modify the behaviour of individuals it is important to recognise that some of the stress can be reduced only by collective action including the development of new organisational approaches to the delivery of water supply and sewerage services.

IV Gardening Practices/Food Production

1 Established areas

The environmental consequence of the present water supply policy under which water was traditionally given a zero price, has been to encourage forms of gardening in both public and private space, which has tended to be devoted to exotic plant and tree species which depend on expensive *scheme* water. Simultaneously we have ignored the possibility of composting and mulching. Furthermore, we have ignored the opportunities for production of more of our own food. Home production of vegetables is currently estimated to be equivalent to 5 per cent of commercial production and domestic hens laid 26 million dozen eggs in the year ending April 1992 (ABS 1994: 1). We have very sketchy information on the level of food production in earlier periods but it is clear that it was much higher when domestic production was more important for the living standard of the average household. Non-metropolitan households account for more home production than those in the State capitals and Melbourne households produce more than Sydney. The higher production in the non-metropolitan areas may be due to less market choice, a local culture favouring home production and better soil conditions. Differences in market choices would not seem to explain the higher production in Melbourne than Sydney but better soil and more favourable growing conditions might. It is obvious that the production of food is limited to those areas with traditional housing.

We should encourage gardening practices which make better use of native species which require less *artificial* watering and encourage composting of kitchen and garden wastes with the resulting material being used to mulch gardens to increase their fertility, reduce their water consumption and increase their capacity to absorb rainfall thus reducing the runoff and the drainage problem. Public gardens and open spaces should, for similar reasons, make greater use of native species.

Large-scale food production in favourable regions together with efficient transport and marketing has reduced the price of food in the cities. Nonetheless, food production should be encouraged to make cities more sustainable and to reduce pressure for monocultural developments in agriculture and slow the *clearance* of more natural bushland. This encouragement might include removing regulatory barriers and creating, encouraging or promoting local seed exchanges and the local exchange, marketing or bartering of surplus production. Gardening for food production or the keeping of hens or other small animals for food will not interest all households at all times, nonetheless, encouraging better husbandry and gardening practices, including the use on site of mulch and composted household and garden wastes for other gardening will achieve similar water savings and reduce drainage. Those who do not like or want to garden either for food production or general amenity should simply pay the full costs of their use of water and the drainage problem they impose on the community.

Tree and shrub planting, especially of *natives*, should be encouraged to help cool the environment in summer, help cope with air pollution and provide habitat for local birds and other fauna. Urban plantations might also be developed to provide fuel for space heating. Although this might increase air pollution in the short run the fact that it is a renewable resource opens the possibility of a fuel demand/supply equilibrium which is closer to neutral in its impact on the environment than the present reliance on fossil fuels. In any event, the use of new efficient combustion chambers for wood burning space heaters rather than open fires will reduce air pollution.

A serious consequence of the increase in housing density arising from current policy is that the greying of the environment resulting from dual occupancy and more extensive medium density housing means there are fewer spaces capable of accommodating such trees. The effect of this is not only a consequential reduction in amenity but a serious loss of the cooling and cleaning effect of trees on their immediate environment and a reduction in their removal of CO_2 close to its point of generation. The cities become even more sharply defined *heat islands* and exaggerated sources of CO_2 which exacerbates the greenhouse effect. A policy to reduce environmental stress would be to encourage growth of trees in the existing areas which in turn means preservation of areas large enough for them to thrive and less encouragement to medium and high density development.

2 New development

The application of natural drainage principles to the design of residential estates and the adoption of grouped housing development practices in which much of the private garden space is developed as communal garden space opens opportunities for new approaches to maintenance of hens and other small animals for food, gardening and tree planting, including trees for fuel. Harvesting and storage of runoff and recycled water could be used to sustain both public and private gardens. If we took a more optimistic view we may find it possible, given the development of appropriate civic attitudes, to develop chicken runs, rabbit hutches and the like, and plant and maintain local orchards to supply households in the development with their own fruit and nuts—this would not obviate the need for orchard areas elsewhere but would take urban areas closer to sustainability.

Residential development can be modified in new developments to facilitate mulching, composting, recycling and reduced runoff while creating high quality space. New occupants can be encouraged and shown how to adopt gardening practices which use mulching and composting to reduce water consumption and increase the production of food or simply to create more environmentally sustainable gardens. These options are, however, not feasible in areas developed to higher than traditional densities.

V Waste Management/Resource Recovery/Recycling

The disposal of solid wastes has been a problem ever since cities developed in Australia. One of the main pressures for a community-based collection and disposal system for coping with domestic wastes was the need to eliminate the practice of discarding wastes on to the street and public places which resulted in unsightly and unhealthy accumulations of *rubbish* or garbage.

In the central areas of the older cities waste disposal was a major problem. Private garbage collection and disposal systems were inadequate so local authorities developed community collection and disposal systems. In Sydney these included transporting solid waste to sea where it was dumped (frequently to reappear as a nuisance on the surf beaches), incineration or tipping at land fill sites. Incineration led to increased air pollution and is now rare although several affluent local authorities in the inner eastern suburbs continue to have their wastes incinerated in Waterloo, a lower income inner southern suburb, to the discomfort and increased health risk for its residents. The inner suburbs quickly ran out of landfill sites.

In the middle and outer local government areas dwellings with their own garden typically managed by composting kitchen and garden wastes or by feeding them to domestic poultry, pigs or pets. Few outer local government authorities organised waste collection until the postwar period. For health reasons the keeping of domestic poultry and pigs was discouraged. Local authorities developed collection and disposal systems based on the use of landfill sites. As the volume of wastes grew it became increasingly difficult to find appropriate sites.

Analysis of the stream of domestic wastes suggests that recycling and composting can reduce the amount going to landfill sites by as much as 70 per cent, greatly prolonging the life of the current tips. About one-third is kitchen and garden waste which can be safely composted or fed to *worm farms* and used as fertiliser and mulch in the garden. Another third consists of material (glass, cans, paper and plastics) that, if separated at source, can be economically recovered and recycled.

A major benefit of this approach is that aerobic composting of this waste results in less environmental stress than disposal via landfill because the latter occurs in anaerobic conditions resulting in the production of methane, which is 21 times more damaging as a greenhouse gas than CO_2. Some of this may be recovered if the landfill site is large enough but it typically is not. The significance of this is that landfill generation of methane is equivalent to approximately 40 per cent of the CO_2 production of all transport. As the major portion of the source of methane from landfill sites is domestic and garden waste and as the great majority of that is in urban areas the policy should be to encourage subdivisions in which blocks are large enough to compost wastes on site. This would enable reduction in methane with the equivalent of up to, say, 20 per cent of the CO_2 production of transport energy consumption which on current estimates exceeds the alleged energy savings resulting from increasing density. We should note, as an aside, that the CO_2 equivalent of agricultural production of methane, mainly from ruminants: sheep and cattle, actually exceeds that from transport. Few proponents of consolidation argue, however, for a major change in our diet as a way of reducing environmental stress.

The form of housing significantly affects the opportunities for the strategy of reducing the stream of wastes to landfill sites. It is virtually impossible for medium to high density housing to compost kitchen wastes because there is little, if any, space to use the resulting mulch. Where the appropriate space is made available and the frequency of collection is high, at-source separation and recovery of glass, paper, cans and plastic can be achieved in most forms of housing although it is easier in the traditional forms of housing development.

The streams of waste from commercial and industrial processes are more likely to be modified and reduced by redesign of the processes carried out in the various commercial and industrial establishments. Pricing policies which included resource rents for water and wood as well as other minerals together with tighter regulations and higher discharge and tipping fees for wastes would encourage such process redesign. In many cases the establishments can more easily cope with their own wastes if they have space near their plant. The wastes from one industrial process may be the material inputs for another. Neither the form of housing nor the structure of the city affects the possibility of resource recovery from industrial processes although the more effectively it is pursued the lower the demand for landfill sites.

The stream of wastes from the construction industry is a significant proportion of the wastes disposed of by landfill. Increasing proportions of materials from demolition of old buildings, especially old houses, are now being recovered and recycled but much more could be. The wastes from construction of new buildings is high and much of it is energy-expensive to manufacture. Greater consideration of the energy costs of construction would lead to greater reuse of existing buildings, the construction of new buildings from less energy-expensive materials and to the more efficient use of materials which would reduce the flow of wastes.

The total stream of domestic wastes can be reduced by minimising the amount of packaging and advertising material. This might be achieved in part by introducing appropriate pricing policies for natural resources and for wastes and by an education program. But this is not a housing and urban development policy although it too would reduce the demand for landfill sites and the production of methane.

The costs of coping with wastes using the traditional landfill processes will become increasingly expensive as sites become more difficult to find and higher standards are set to control leachates to minimise the impact of wastes disposal on the water table or on natural drainage catchments. The introduction of charges related to the volume and type of wastes collected from different types of development would make the population more aware of the costs of waste disposal and of its impact on the environment. Housing forms that allow residents to minimise the wastes transported from their property should be encouraged.

1 Existing development

Instead of paying for waste collection services as part of the general charge for local services through property-based rates, waste collection services should be charged for by the volume and type of waste collected. Residents should be encouraged to separate out those wastes that can be recovered and recycled, compost and mulch those that can be handled on site, and thus reduce the volume to be transported to tips. Most areas of traditional residential development can cope with their own kitchen and garden wastes by composting but this is not a viable option for the great proportion of medium to high density housing. The costs of waste collection should, however, be borne by those who create the problem.

Industrial and commercial undertakings may also find their sites too cramped to redesign their processes to reduce waste production or process it on site. Nonetheless, waste disposal pricing related to volume and type of waste is more likely to encourage industry and commerce to separate out their wastes for recycling and to re-examine their processes and practices to reduce waste.

2 New development

There are more opportunities at traditional density in new developments. New residential developments can be designed with composting facilities which can even include composting toilets. The composts can be used as mulch on gardens. It may even be attractive to introduce *environmental covenants* on residential developments to ensure that residents become sensitive to the need to reduce wastes and to cope with as much of it on site as possible. This option is less feasible in the higher density developments.

Commercial and shopping centres can be developed with facilities which make it easier to separate and recycle materials. Industrial plant can be developed to reduce the waste stream by coping with more of it on site.

Higher density development limits the capacity of residential and industrial areas to cope with a high proportion of their wastes because there is less land that is not covered by buildings or hard surfaces. The fact that denser developments require more of the wastes of urban activities to be collected and transported to large processing sites increases environmental stress.

VI Noise Pollution

Noise is one of those externalities of urban development which reduces the amenity of urban living. Noise may come from the busy hum of a factory, the hubbub of music and conversation from a cafe, the incessant driving beat of a disco but it is more likely to come from the pervasive intrusive sounds of traffic or, in the case of Sydney, from the airport. The amenity of an area may be affected by its ambient noise level, which is frequently that of the traffic passing through. If the levels are excessive, noise may injuriously affect the health of residents. There is little data relating to the ambient noise levels of different forms of development although it is clear that noise is one of the sources of friction among residents of medium density housing. Noise can reduce the privacy of an area. Whether an area is regarded as *quiet, peaceful* or *tranquil* is regarded as a positive feature by real estate agents gives some clues as to the value the market places on such an attribute. This condition is more likely to be found in traditional residential areas than in medium density developments. The denser the development the more likely the sounds of traffic, police sirens, fire engines and of trains will be reflected and reverberate producing the familiar noise of the city. Lower density development allows the sounds from the individual sources to attenuate without being intrusive.

A variety of strategies is available to reduce noise or to reduce its invasiveness but each strategy has a cost. Ambient noise can be excluded from medium and high density housing by appropriate insulation, including double glazing of windows, but this is expensive and is an option only open to those who can afford the cost. One cost usually associated with this strategy is that windows must be kept closed—which of course is a limitation not lightly countenanced—you can live in an environment which is unhealthily stuffy but still be able to enjoy the delicate notes of a Beethoven sonata untortured by the muffled roar of the traffic. Some reduction in noise can be achieved by modifications to the vehicles themselves but usually at the cost of increased weight.

Airport noise can be made less intrusive by limiting the number and times of aircraft movements, by insulating buildings including dwellings, by modifying the aircraft or by shifting the airports. Limiting aircraft movements does not reduce peak level but might make the noise *bearable*. Insulating against noise is expensive and carries with it costs alluded to above. Modifications to aircraft and their engines has been effective but is expensive and has reached a technological barrier at present. Shifting airports away from built up areas is the most effective method but few governments have been prepared to introduce the planning mechanisms to service the necessary separation or to make the appropriate investment in airports.

VII Air Pollution

Air pollution is a serious problem in Australian cities. The amount of air pollution is a function of the nature and scale of activities carried out in the cities and especially with the energy consumption associated with them, which we discuss later. There are, however, two aspects of the form of the city that bear on air pollution which we briefly discuss here.

The first relates to the mixed development. One reason factories were and remain separated from residential areas is that many processes resulted in release of particulates and gases which were offensive, injurious to health and damaging to property or toxic even if they were not greenhouse gases. Most of the dust and grit deposited on households from factory emissions may not have been injurious to health, or contributed to the greenhouse effect but they added to the discomfitures of life and the cost of cleanliness for those nearby. The smell of chocolates being made or the malting of barley may conjure up pleasurable responses but living near to a chocolate factory or a brewery can be intolerably invasive. The increasing incidence of allergy illnesses of people may well be related to the release into the atmosphere of various gaseous emissions from industrial and commercial processes (although dietary and lifestyle factors may also be significant). There is no reason to believe that, improvements in industrial processes and monitoring notwithstanding, there will be no accidental release of offensive, health-damaging or toxic gases nor that changes in the processes carried out at a particular site can be controlled in such a way that there will be no increase in the risk of the release of offensive, health-damaging or toxic gases in the future. We cannot even be sure that commercial and industrial establishments that use no toxic products today will so continue tomorrow. Given that the land use controls currently employed crudely group activities and are not updated frequently to account for changes in the practices and processes in the establishments in particular industries, consolidation resulting in higher density development in which industrial or commercial processes are allowed in residential areas simply increases the risk of such exposure. The prudent response would be to continually update the standards for emissions (and enforce them) and to continue to separate industrial and commercial uses from residential areas.

A second source of air pollution is that which comes from the conscription of residents in the olfactory delights of neighbours' meals or activities. Living near a restaurant or even a sidewalk cafe can result in exposure to the brewing of coffee or the preparation of a cabbage dish which all do not find pleasing all the time. Similar invasions of privacy may be experienced by households living at medium to high density when they can tell from the breeze that their neighbours are about to feast on some aromatic dish. These experiences are rare in traditional housing developments. The lower density allows most of these exhausts to dissipate to low or non-irritating levels.

VIII Energy Consumption

Energy consumption is an important source of stress to the environment because of the release to the environment of waste heat and the products of combustion or conversion of the energy (ozone, CO_2, CO, NO_X, SO_2) from fossil fuels like coal and petroleum products. These gases have two effects: on the local environment and, on global climate change—the greenhouse effect.

The local effects of these products of consumption may include photochemical smog induced by the ozone, increase in damage to buildings and plant life from the SO_2 producing acid rain and greater exposure of the population to gases which are known carcinogens.

The most important global climate change or greenhouse gas generated by energy consumption is CO_2. Other gases are important but for the purpose of this discussion we confine ourselves to consideration of CO_2 which we take as the indicator of the greenhouse effect.

The greater proportion of the energy is consumed in urban areas either at fixed point sites in the production or creation of the urban environment and in the operation of the city or in mobile sources of consumption as its inhabitants pursue their interests and activities. The fixed point sources are all the dwellings, factories, offices, shops, and so on which make up the fabric of the city. The mobile sources are all the forms of transport.

IX Fixed Point Sources

The shares of the primary fuel types in Australian energy consumption for 1991–1992 are set out in Table 3.2. Renewable energy accounts for only 6 per cent, all of which is used at fixed points of consumption. The greater part of the 94 per cent of non-renewable energy sources is consumed at fixed points. Virtually all the coal and the greater proportion of the natural gas is consumed at fixed points, mostly being converted to electricity for final use at yet another fixed point, mostly in the city.

Table 3.2

Shares of the Primary Fuel Types in Energy Consumption in 1991-1992

Petroleum Products	36%
Black Coal	29%
Natural Gas	17%
Brown Coal	12%
Renewables	6%

Source: Bush, S, Leonard, M, Bowen, B, Jones, B, Donaldson, K, & Ho Trieu, L, 1993, *Energy Demand and Supply Projections: Australia 1992-1993 to 2004-2005*, Australian Bureau of Agriculture and Resource Economics, Research Report 93.2 Canberra.

X Production of the Built Environment

A significant proportion of the energy consumed in Australia is used in the manufacture of building materials, their fabrication into components and fittings and in the construction of buildings. Our knowledge of the energy costs or the energy embodied in different forms or types of buildings is sketchy. Tucker, Salomonsson and Macsporran (1994) estimate that there is a total of 22,500 petajoules (PJ) of embodied energy invested in the national building stock, which is nine years of total national energy consumption and of which 10,200 PJ is in the residential building stock. Tucker and Treloar (1994: 4) further estimate that "[T]he CO_2 emitted over the years in stock production . . . was estimated to be approximately 2200Mt [million tonnes]". If the building stock is growing by 1 per cent per annum and the average life is 100 years that would mean 450 PJ per annum was being used. We can only guess at how much of this carbon was *fixed* by the subsequent or replacement growth of trees and we have no reliable estimate of what proportion of annual consumption of energy is embodied in the built environment. That is, we have no reliable estimates of what might be the amount of energy *invested* annually in the physical capital of urban areas, the built environment, or the equivalent amount of CO_2 emitted and how much is fixed by replacement tree growth. Tucker & Treloar (1994: 7) claim, however, that "[T]he activity in the construction sectors is one of the main contributors to energy consumption and CO_2 emissions nationally."

We can therefore only hint at directions we might need to take to minimise energy consumption involved in developing and replacing the building stock of the city. Holland & Holland (1991), however, report that weatherboard houses embody one-sixth the energy of brick veneer houses of the same thermal resistance and that timber framed houses *store* 7.5 tonnes of carbon whereas steel framed houses release 2.9 tonnes to the atmosphere. That is, timber houses are less environmentally stressful than houses using significant amounts of steel or bricks.

One environmentally friendly approach would be to return to more labour intensive methods of construction including the use of stone. Currently, traditional forms of low density housing are usually built from wood and clay bricks or concrete blocks. They may be built from *natural* materials such as stone, rammed earth or wood which embody relatively little energy.

Multi-storey housing is usually built from materials which are more energy expensive. Structural requirements and considerations of fire safety and privacy generally dictate the use of bricks, reinforced concrete and steel in buildings over two storeys. For buildings over three storeys only bricks, reinforced concrete or steel may be used and their embodied energy may be higher than the energy required to operate them for the whole of their life.

The embodied energy in office buildings may be extremely high. One study of a 15-storey office block in Melbourne reported by

Holland & Holland (1991) showed that, over a 40-year period, its embodied energy exceeded its operating energy. The embodied energy of high rise housing is also likely to be very high relative to its operation because of the higher level of investment in fixtures and fittings.

The energy embodied in existing buildings is a sunk cost so the focus of energy efficiency policy must be on new development and on the refurbishment of existing buildings; their demolition to permit them to be replaced requires the sacrifice of most of the energy which was embodied in them when constructed and should therefore be undertaken only as a last resort.

In addition to the energy embodied in a building a significant proportion of energy consumed in the construction phase is in the waste generated during construction. Some of this waste is in the form of off-cuts of timber, plaster board, insulation, broken bricks, formwork and packaging and so on. More off site fabrication of components and building elements can reduce wastage from off-cuts and so on but the wastage is still significant.

The strategy should be to encourage low embodied energy forms of housing and commercial buildings and to encourage methods of construction which minimise waste production. This would lead to the recycling of existing buildings, encouragement of timber dwellings and of low rise commercial buildings using factory produced components. Replacement of low rise development with high density or high rise buildings, which is implicit in consolidation policy, is expensive in terms of embodied energy and as a result adds to environmental stress.

> Demolition of buildings which have not outlived their physical life should be regarded as an 'environmentally unfriendly' activity, in the context of embodied energy and resultant CO_2 emissions. (Tucker & Treloar 1994: 7)

XI Operation of the Built Environment

A significant proportion of the energy consumed in Australia is consumed in the day-to-day operation or recurrent energy costs of urban areas. Some of this consumption might be influenced by the form or structure of the city and some is related to the lifestyle choices, recreation and consumption of residents and their activities including employment and production. The following discussion is necessarily imprecise but it provides some firm indications of the kinds of policies or behavioural changes which would be necessary to reduce environmental stress from both existing and new development.

1 Existing development

The major ways energy is consumed are heating and cooling in industrial, commercial and domestic activities (including space heating), lighting and water heating.

We have known for some time how to reduce the costs of space heating and cooling, especially in dwellings, but there has been great reluctance to design and construct buildings to maximise passive heating or to reduce the heat load in summer. Design has been more sensitive to short-term costs of construction than long term operating costs. Whole-of-life energy costs have rarely been considered.

Some reduction in the energy consumption of existing buildings could be achieved by small modifications to the ventilation of the older dwellings to reduce heat loss and by reducing draughts around doors and windows and by educating households to operate their dwellings at lower winter temperatures or to use less or lower temperature hot water. In some cases it may be efficient to install solar heating for water heating but this will probably only be economically feasible when existing water heaters and storage need to be replaced. In other cases it may be efficient to install better insulation in walls, ceilings and floors. In most cases, however, significant improvement in energy efficiency of existing buildings is very expensive.

In larger buildings, especially offices and the larger apartment blocks, better energy management programs for the building as a whole can lead to significant energy savings. Similarly, better energy management and the redesign of manufacturing processes can result in significant energy savings.

Housing

The design, construction, orientation and use of dwellings have developed with little concern for energy consumption. Australia's early housing was heavily influenced by the practices and conventions which the original settlers brought with them as part of their cultural baggage. Few concessions were made to the Australian climate. Later, in different regions, housing styles developed which were more appropriate but since energy costs were low, design of housing took little account of its use. Housing designs were just as subject to *fashion* as in many other areas of urban life and the influence of *modern* ideas, especially from the United States of America led to the widespread development of the *Californian bungalow*—a design which was not particularly sensible in Australian conditions since it afforded little protection from the sun nor was it designed for efficient heating. Households did not expect to heat their whole house. During the cooler period of the year household life took place in the warmer spaces of dwellings and household members dressed accordingly. Houses were, in any event, hard to heat because the influence of miasmatic theories of disease transmission in the late nineteenth century led to building regulations which required rooms to be continuously ventilated. More recently, the freedom promised by *clean* cheap fuel, the development of easily installed ducted heating systems, increasing living standards and the modernisation of regulations has been reflected in the development of more open plan housing. Energy consumption has risen.

Claims are made that the energy costs of the traditional form of housing are too high and that alternative higher density development would lead to great energy savings in the operation of dwellings. The implicit reason is that the form of housing affects the level of essential energy consumption. Whether this is a valid claim depends first on the way the occupants of different forms of housing actually use their dwellings, which determines annual energy consumption, the form of energy they use and on the net use of embodied energy in the demolition of the existing housing and its replacement with higher embodied energy dwellings is energy efficient.

Household expenditure survey information reveals that the expenditure on energy is greater for conventional houses than for high or low rise flats (Table 3.3). When these figures are adjusted for household size, expenditure per head is higher in the higher density housing. But it is also higher per capita the smaller the household size, regardless of dwelling type.

Table 3.3

Average Weekly Expenditure on Total Fuel and Power 1988 - 1989

Type of Dwelling	Average Weekly Expenditure per Household[a]	Average Weekly Expenditure per Person[b]
Separate House	13.9	4.6
Flat or Apartment	9.0	5.0
Semi Detached	10.0	4.8
Caravan	8.4	4.7
Other	10.5	3.7
Total	12.9	4.9

Source: Australian Bureau of Statistics 1992, *Housing Australia: A Statistical Overview*, ABS Cat No 1320.0 (unpublished data from the 1988–1989 Household Expenditure Survey); 1991 Census of Population and Housing, Basic Community Profile, Cat No 2722.0.

Note: (a) Estimates are based on data collected in the 1988–1989 Household Expenditure Survey; (b) an adjustment for expenditure per person was derived by dividing average weekly household expenditure on total fuel and power by an estimate (based on the 1991 census of population and housing) of the average number of persons per type of occupied private dwelling.

A problem with the data is that it is not disaggregated by city although *Housing Australia* (ABS 1992: 42) suggests that Canberra, Melbourne and Hobart have the highest average expenditure on fuel and power which is certainly due to their higher consumption of energy for space heating. Unpublished data from the 1988–1989 Household Expenditure Survey reported in *Housing Australia* (ABS 1992: 91) indicates that households in separate houses which they own outright spend less on fuel and power than those who are still paying them off. We note that households who have paid off their houses are usually smaller, have lower incomes and are older. Those households in their own high and low rise flats spend more than those still paying off their flats whereas those who own their own *semis* pay less than those still paying them off. Renters tend to spend less on fuel and power than owners. There may be a relationship between income or wealth and expenditure on total fuel and power, that is, there may be a relationship between income and wealth and discretionary energy consumption in a manner similar to other expenditure patterns but this is not clear from the data presented. We should note, as an aside, that on average households spend less on fuel and power than on alcoholic beverages (1.9 per cent of total household expenditure compared with 2.5 per cent) and that they spend almost six times as much on all transport (11.3 per cent—not all of which is on energy and includes plane travel) as they do on fuel and power. What proportion of transport expenditure is on public compared with private transport is not clear. According to estimates of the 1988–1989 Household Expenditure Survey, the average weekly household expenditure on public transport was about 0.4 per cent of all household expenditure.

Separate houses consume more reticulated energy than medium density housing or flats. The energy consumed in separate houses is more likely to come from a wider variety of forms than in flats. High rise flats are more likely to use electricity for all their energy needs whereas houses are more likely to use renewable sources such as wood and solar power for a significant proportion of their needs. Households in semi-detached housing (including row/terrace houses and townhouses) spend nearly as much on energy as those in separate houses and it is again more likely to be as electricity or natural gas. This inconclusive exploration of energy consumption and expenditure suggests that there is no strong relationship between form of housing and energy consumption. But the fact that households spend so little of their income on fuel and power suggests that they would be loath to spend large sums on altering their dwellings to achieve greater energy efficiency. This could change if fuel and energy prices were increased to include resource rent components or if an energy tax such as a carbon tax was levied.

Commercial buildings

Until recently commercial buildings, including offices, relied on a supply of cheap, often subsidised, energy. Offices, especially the high rise constructions of the central city, are built from materials which are energy intensive to manufacture and fabricate. More importantly, however, the buildings are designed in such a way that they cannot function without the continuous consumption of large amounts of energy for heating, cooling and air conditioning. Moreover, they need a lot of energy to operate lifts. For a variety of reasons, including safety and local air pollution, high rise buildings whether for offices or residences can use only the more expensive forms of energy for their operation, although gas is predominantly used for water heating. Electricity is the most expensive in terms of its environmental impact.

Industrial plants

Apart from improving the insulation of factory buildings and reducing energy loss through poorly fitted doors and windows the most significant reductions in energy consumption can come through redesign of processes and activities carried out. Although each light uses relatively little energy the need to properly illuminate factories means they have many lights leading to high total consumption of electricity. The new more energy efficient lighting that can be fitted in existing fixtures will lead to reductions in energy consumption in most industrial fields.

2 New Development

Although opportunities for reduction in energy consumption in existing developments appear to be limited, the opportunities are much greater in new development. In most parts of Australia buildings can be designed to efficiently make use of solar heating for water for domestic, public, commercial and industrial purposes. It is easier to introduce efficiencies in the levels of both essential and discretionary consumption of energy in new development. We may also be approaching the point where it is economical to use solar arrays in the cladding of residential and commercial buildings to harvest solar energy converted to electrical energy for their operational energy needs.

Buildings, including dwellings, can be designed to take better account of the local climate for their heating, cooling and lighting. In some regions this will require that they be designed to ensure maximum protection from the sun in summer and to minimise the use of materials which increase the heat load on the building. They can also be designed to make maximum use of natural cooling and ventilation.

In colder regions where buildings must be heated in winter they can be oriented to *trap* as much winter solar energy as possible. That is, appropriate design and siting as well as the use of the appropriate materials in their construction can result in significant gains in efficiency through the passive heating of buildings. In some regions all the space heating needs of buildings can be met in this way. The only caveat is that to achieve these economies the buildings need to be operated so that curtains are drawn when the sun goes off the windows and that openings are closed to keep the heat in. The way buildings are used significantly affects the extent to which the designed efficiencies are realised.

In principle these measures can apply to existing development but the efficiencies can be more easily attained in new developments because they can be readily incorporated in their construction. The adage that "[G]ood design costs no more than poor" can also be applied to construction. Energy efficiencies may be able to be attained in good quality construction but rarely are in poor, which may be just as expensive. To achieve the efficiencies in energy consumption, however, may require changes in attitude to building location and functional layout. Changing new dwelling subdivision and dwelling designs so that they are oriented in relation to the sun rather than the street probably requires the population to be educated away from the socially determined values of aspect and *show* or conspicuous consumption to give more weight to considerations of energy efficiency. The population needs to be shown that to achieve energy efficiency dwellings should be oriented so that they capture more of the sun's rays during the cooler months and have windows shaded during the hotter months rather than have the dwellings oriented to the street.

Although many new buildings are now designed with energy efficiency in mind and often have insulation installed when they are being constructed, few studies have been undertaken to see whether the efficiency sought has been achieved: we do not know whether the quality of construction has been of high enough standard to minimise losses due to gaps around windows and doors or to confirm that the wall, ceiling and floor insulation has been installed to achieve the designed savings. Failure to achieve economies may be due to the quality of supervision and workmanship—buildings may be designed to be more thermally efficient and the appropriate materials may actually be used in their construction but unless the materials are properly installed there may be little gain in operational efficiency of the building. The tendency for developers to try to retain tight control over costs tends to militate against quality of workmanship because of the temptation to *cut corners*. Better, non-destructive testing techniques allied with payment based on quality performance assessed by independent arbitrators would help achieve greater energy efficiency in the construction of buildings.

We also have had few post occupancy studies to determine whether the buildings are actually used in a manner that achieves their design efficiency. Housing may be designed to be energy efficient, especially those designs which rely on passive solar heating, but if people are not home to close the openings and draw the curtains when the sun goes off the windows the heat captured or stored will be quickly lost. New *smart* windows which can minimise the heat loss may obviate the need for this change in behaviour although they are more expensive in energy terms to produce.

Changes in gardening practices and tree planting can lead to significant savings of energy both in heating and cooling buildings and public spaces. Again, these efficiencies are more easily achieved in new than in existing development.

Lower density development might experience greater heat losses but it is more likely to be able to meet its energy needs using renewable sources such as wood and can take better advantage of solar energy than higher density development.

XII Mobile Sources: Transport and Communication

The second major use of energy in cities is in transport. The demand for transport is derived from the demand to do different things at different places daily, weekly or annually, and to produce, process and consume goods at different places. People use transport to travel between their homes and work and to engage in commerce and their wide range of recreational and cultural activities. Firms use energy in the transport involved in transacting their business, contacting and servicing customers and clients, conveying the raw materials to their factories and products to markets.

Much of the research directed at the relationship between the journey to work and the form of urban development implicitly assumes this to be *essential* and the policy recommendations based on the alleged relationship between density or urban form and transport energy consumption are founded on that assumption. Less focus is given to the relationship between business travel and urban form even though it could also be regarded as essential. The small amount of energy used because some enjoy the kinaesthetic delights of travel might be regarded unambiguously as *discretionary* and uninfluenced by the form of the city. The great proportion of transport energy is used for more banal purposes such as shopping, recreation and cultural activities. Much of this consumption can be regarded as uninfluenced by urban form.

How can people have access to their wide range of interests and activities and firms pursue their operations while minimising movement around the city? If households can satisfy their needs for mobility by organising the distribution of their destinations so that they have wide choices in employment, commercial, cultural and recreational activities close to where they live they could reduce their need to travel. But this is the paradox which many policy makers fail to recognise. Propinquity or location is only one element in the generation of travel. Enhanced mobility gives people greater access to a wider range of interests and activities and allows them a higher degree of engagement with other like-minded members of the various communities to which they belong, thus enriching their lives and contributing to social and economic vitality. The notion that people will be prepared to accept a circumscribed range of interests by confining their travel to public transport or only to those activities within easy reach of their homes is a fundamental misunderstanding of their desires and their willingness to bear the cost of satisfying those desires (reflected in the fact that they spend, on average, such a high proportion of their income on transport) and is not supported by evidence of their behaviour.

Transport, and specifically the use of the motor car, has become the major environmental consideration in the debate over urban form. All other environmental issues or sources of environmental stress are virtually ignored. Commentators refer to the *dominance of the car* as though the car has some independent intelligence. Although we might be able to develop cars with artificial intelligence those on the streets today and in the immediate future are simply pieces of technology employed by people in the pursuit of their various interests. The central problem on which commentators, activists and politicians should focus is the pollution resulting from the operation of internal combustion engines. What would their attitude to private transport be if we had a form of motive power in cars which did not produce greenhouse gases or did so at acceptable levels? Undoubtedly, while we would still have accidents, noise and visual pollution, cars that did not pollute would change the dynamics of the debate although it is clear that, in spite of their undeniable attractions, some would still argue that the use of private forms of transport should be discouraged because of what they would claim were the benefits of collective behaviour.

But we should take a step back. We should ask what is the context and scale of the problem?

Of the petroleum products used in Australia about 61 per cent are consumed in the road transport sector which uses about 22 per cent of total energy consumption. This corresponds closely with Naughten et al (1993) who estimate that 24 per cent of CO_2 emissions comes from road transport.

How do we estimate how much of this consumption of petroleum products arising from road transport occurs in the city? How much of it is *essential* and affected by urban form? A report prepared for the Victorian Strategic Transport Study (VSTS) in 1992 implied that about 60 per cent of all road transport in Victoria was in the Melbourne metropolitan area.

The Bureau of Transport and Communications Economics (1991b) estimates that cars accounted for as much as 88 per cent of energy used in urban passenger transport in 1988. In Sydney 65 per cent of commuter travel was by private car while 30 per cent was by public transport.

Table 3.4

Total Kilometres Travelled by Type of Vehicle and Purpose: Australia: Twelve Months Ended 30 September 1991

Type of Vehicle	Business	Total to and from Work	Private	Total
		million kilometres		
Passenger Vehicles	25,956.6	29,057.2	59,316.8	114,286.2
Motor Cycles	165.7	643.1	806	1614.8
Light Commercial Vehicles	13,554.8	4489.6	4769.2	22,813.6
Rigid Trucks	5751.5	248.5	113.5	6113.6
Articulated Trucks	3929.2	25.6	4.3	3959.1
Other Truck Types	196.1	2.6	2.2	200.9
Buses	1320.9	27.9	51.9	1400.7
Total	50,874.9	34,494.5	65,063.9	150,388.7
		per cent		
Passenger Vehicles	22.7	25.4	52.0	76.0
Motor Cycles	10.3	39.8	50.0	1.1
Light Commercial Vehicles	59.4	19.7	21.0	15.2
Rigid Trucks	94.1	4.1	1.7	4.1
Articulated Trucks	99.2	0.7	0.1	2.6
Other Truck Types	97.6	1.3	1.1	0.1
Buses	94.3	2.0	3.7	0.9
Total	33.8	23.0	43.3	100.00

Source: Australian Bureau of Statistics, Cat No 9208.0, Survey of Motor Vehicle Use: Australia, 30 September 1991, Table 9.

Note: percentages may not total to 100 because of decimal rounding.

The 1991 Survey of Motor Vehicle Use shows (Table 3.4) that a third of all road travel in Australia is for business and approximately a half of this is by passenger vehicles (cars). About 23 per cent of all travel by road is for journeys to or from work, that is, commuter travel, with more than a quarter of all car travel being for that purpose. That is, about 57 per cent of all road travel could be regarded as *essential* consumption which potentially could be influenced by urban form. But whether more than a small reduction could be achieved is not clear. The costs of achieving the reduction in terms of destruction and replacement of embodied energy costs would be high and would probably significantly outweigh any marginal transport energy savings.

If we assume that the distribution of road travel is similar in the city to that in Australia as a whole and we make the further simplifying assumption that the greenhouse gases generated per kilometre of travel are the same for all vehicle types (trucks and buses generate more than cars and motor cycles less) we can estimate that the journey to or from work in the city by road transport is equivalent to about 3.4 per cent of total CO_2 production (0.23 x 0.24 x 0.61). This gives an upper estimate of the reduction in greenhouse gas (CO_2) emission which could theoretically be obtained by transferring *all* journeys to or from work in the city by road transport to some alternative form of transport. This is a crude estimate because, even if it were desirable and could be achieved, the alternative modes of transport would also consume energy, usually leading to the production of greenhouse gases.

The policy of consolidation is often justified on the grounds that it reduces the journey to work and, by implication, air pollution. It is also predicated on the assumption that more of these journeys would be transferred from private cars to public transport. By implication the assumption is that non-work journeys would also be reduced. None of the proponents of the policy make any estimate of the reduction in the length of journey to or from work or for other trip purposes which they claim would follow from consolidation, nor do they provide any estimate of the reduction in greenhouse gases which they claim would follow from transfer from cars to public transport. That is, they provide no estimate of the reductions in either *essential* or *discretionary* transport energy consumption, which they claim would arise from a change in urban form.

It is interesting to note that in spite of increasing vehicle registrations and transport energy consumption in New South Wales over the period 1980 to 1992, the number of days in Sydney with a low pollution index increased, the number of days on which the photochemical smog exceeded the National Health and Medical Research Council (NHMRC) goal fell, lead pollution fell and the number of days per year on which the visibility goal was exceeded fell (New South Wales Department of Transport 1995). That is, in spite of the claims that the traditional form of development of Sydney is environmentally stressful, the accepted measures for transport-related pollution indicate it has actually fallen—before the consolidation policy can have had such an effect.

In reviewing the plethora of studies designed to show how increasing the density of urban areas would reduce travel, Breheny (1992) came to the conclusion that it would not.

The distribution of the journey to work suggests that in Sydney only 17 per cent work in the CBD, 35 per cent work in the local government area in which they live and the remainder work throughout the metropolitan area. The sketchy evidence available indicates that, on average, the journey to work is remarkably stable in terms of length or time taken. Those who work in the CBD appear to have experienced a slight increase in the length of their journeys (but a high proportion of them already travel by public transport); this has been offset to some degree by a fall in the length of work journeys of those who work locally or who travel to non-central locations. The 48 per cent of the workforce working in locations distributed throughout the metropolitan area have work journeys which are highly circumferential. Neither the fixed track highly centralised public transport system nor the radial road system facilitate these journeys. Brotchie et al (1995) conclude that the most effective way of meeting the demand for circumferential travel would be to build circumferential freeways.

We could imagine a situation where more people were encouraged to walk or cycle to local employment. While this would tend to reduce the journey to work it would not have a major effect on car travel or usage. A high proportion of local employment is already taken up by local people so that we cannot expect a great reduction of work trips without a massive change in the distribution of jobs. There is no indication that we can expect such a rearrangement of employment, nor, given the benefit from separation of industrial and much commercial activity from residential areas, should policy be directed to achieve it. Changing urban form by increasing density is unlikely to affect the employment distribution or the propensity of people to travel to work by public transport.

In the major cities we have seen a reduction in the proportion of the workforce engaged in the functions discharged in their central areas. In some cases we have seen a reduction in the absolute numbers employed in the central areas. These absolute and relative reductions have occurred as a result of a variety of economic and social processes and there is no reason to believe that these processes will be reversed, so we cannot expect the great refocusing of jobs in the central areas which would be necessary for an increase in public transport patronage.

Most of the debate over travel focuses on journeys to and from work yet more than half of all travel by cars is for *private* trips for cultural, recreational and shopping activities.

What can we make of these facts? The first and most obvious point is that attempts to limit the use of the car would seriously affect the way business is conducted. The second is that it would seriously affect the way goods and materials are transported. We can expect that further developments in information technology will lead to more business being conducted or arranged through this medium but it is inconceivable that modern business can be conducted without some form of private transport. The organisation of production, the close connection between production and retailing together with the organisation of the entry and distribution of imports and the collection and assembly of exports now relies to a large extent on the transport by road of goods and people. It is inconceivable that Australian cities can now be operated without a major and efficient road transport system.

One of the preoccupations of commentators on the city is the congestion which is sometimes evident in the road system. The simple conclusion is drawn that the congestion in peak periods arises from people trying to get to and from jobs in the centre. Further, it is assumed that congestion is a pathological condition whereas it simply reflects intensive use of scarce road space. Much of the congestion arises because the highly centralised road system funnels traffic that has other destinations through the city centre. The fact that much of the peak traffic is not work related is also overlooked. The reality is that even the most congested points in the road system are congested for only part of the time and most elements in the road system are rarely congested.

There is no case for complacency nor can we be sanguine about the future but the recent history of the car indicates that it has improved in efficiency dramatically over the past 20 years. The BTCE (1991) study indicates that as car ownership levels off and as the vehicle fleet continues to become more efficient, Australia will experience a fall in its greenhouse gas emissions from this source. Continued improvement in efficiency of internal combustion engines can reasonably be expected to occur and we can expect that cars will be made lighter. Improvements in both the engines and the bodies of cars will further reduce greenhouse gas emissions from cars. In addition the development of new forms of motive power can be expected to produce even smaller emission levels (Boethius 1995a). There must also be some opportunities to improve the efficiency of the transport of goods and services which would result in lower energy consumption. But for goods transport that choice is less available, though the Australian economy is becoming less goods intensive. Some of these small reductions in transport energy consumption might relate to improvements in layout and circulation.

Communities should at all times endeavour to find ways of pursuing their interests and activities in ways which minimise environmental stress. Stress from the kinds of technologies employed in transport should not be ignored in this endeavour. The question which arises is: how can a community pursue its interests and retain the freedom to travel when and where its members wish without creating environmental stress? It seems clear that trying to limit choices of when and where to travel simply reduces the welfare of the population. Some technologies such as tele-commuting can be used to minimise work travel but it seems that because people are social creatures they have a strong need for a high level of interactions with others and to *know* their environment, to develop a familiarity with their cities which can come only from travel in and exploration of them. In any event, to the extent that tele-commuting becomes more widespread and people spend more time working in and from their homes they will want more space both in and around their homes to make themselves more comfortable. Moreover, an increase in tele-commuting would weaken the argument for concentration or consolidation because it would tend to reduce the demand for central city work travel. We cannot expect more than a small proportion of people to adopt telecommuting so this will not be the source of a significant reduction in travel.

There are some clues as to the direction we might take. The modern car uses about 20 per cent less petrol per kilometre travelled than models of just 20 years ago. Even with these new levels of efficiency car engines are still only at most about 20 per cent efficient. We could pursue improved engine efficiency and that could lead to reduced greenhouse gas emission. There is some reason to believe that we will achieve new higher levels of efficiency (Boethius 1995). This is no reason for us to be sanguine about petrol powered cars. But there are other possibilities.

This writer is not proposing a technologically determined solution to the problem of environmental stress associated with the present form of motive power in cars. But there is some indication that with the right kinds of social attitudes, political processes and regulatory framework allied with appropriate market responses we can develop forms of private transport which produce less greenhouse gas than present vehicles without changing the form of our cities.

XIII Management of Demand and Car Usage

The focus of consolidation policy has been to try to moderate demand for travel by changing the form of urban areas. Very little attention has been directed at changing the structure of urban areas. Yet it appears that this feature of cities determines their efficiency. One response to the amount of energy consumed by transport would be to try to reshape the demand by relocating destinations. The first and most obvious initiative would be to try to harness the processes which are already occurring in our urban areas and developing them as *sets* of connected centres. Some of the centres would be centres for industrial production and service industry. Others would be foci of retailing, commerce and public administration. Ideally these centres would be connected by a well-developed public transport system (not necessarily fixed rail). The decentralisation of retailing, commerce and public administration would also need to be accompanied by a cultural development policy which ensured that investment in cultural and recreational facilities were developed in and as part of each of the centres.

Most urban development policies articulated by State governments have included statements of commitment to the notion of the development of sub-centres. Although there has been a substantial amount of decentralised development, the policies have failed. Part of the reason is that while the private sector has *read* the demand for decentralised retailing and cultural activities and some parts of the private sector have changed their labour practices and restructured and decentralised their manufacturing and other operations, governments have not been prepared to vigorously implement their own policies. Governments have not acted to achieve the synergies which were possible in the decision of the private sector to relocate their activities or to develop them away from the traditional centres. They have always been able to rationalise their failure to disallow proposals for particular development in the city centre on the grounds that if the development was not allowed there it would be made outside the city or State concerned.

The development of the sub-centres requires a higher degree of government intervention in controlling the location of investment. It also needs to be accompanied by an appropriate degree of decentralisation of administration and devolution of political power. That is, to reinforce the functioning of the sub-centres and make them more identifiable and more relevant to the lives of residents it would be appropriate to ensure that they were the centres of relatively powerful local government. The same rationale would apply to the development of regional centres.

Research into travel time budgets suggests that most people expect to have to undertake a journey from their home to their place of work. They might even find it desirable for a variety of reasons to separate their domestic life from their working domain. Their propensity to limit their journey to work and also to work locally would make the development of sub-centres a desirable planning policy. The development of centres with a wide range of retailing, employment and cultural activities would not only exploit the opportunity to reduce the journey to work but also reduce the length of trips for other activities.

Another means of encouraging the development of sub-centres would be to introduce pricing and regulatory policies designed to shorten trips and or to discourage them from the CBD and focus them on the suburban centres. Location and time specific road pricing is now technically feasible and could be used to reduce congestion by charging for the use of roads at the most congested times in the most congested places. Tollways may be profitable investments for the governments or corporations which own them but they do not give the right kinds of signals if the objective is to manage demand on the transport system in the most efficient way. The introduction of road pricing would need to be associated with a major reduction of taxes on fuel. Taxes on fuel might still be levied, however, first as part of environment policy, and secondly as a general revenue measure and thirdly to fund rural roads programs. That component of the present taxes which is justified as a charge for urban road use to fund investment and operating costs would be replaced by road user charges. These charges would provide the necessary differential feedback information which would allow users to respond to the costs of their trips including the costs they impose on others. That is, the charges would be high enough to lead some users of roads in highly congested areas at highly congested times to modify their behaviour to reduce their costs.

Such prices would be set by the communities which bear the costs of congestion and the responsibility for providing roads. They would thus be charges set at State and local government level and could be expected to result in changes to the location decisions of individuals and firms. Introduction of such charges would have the incidental effect of allowing the Commonwealth to withdraw from expenditure on State road programs. States and regions would then get the roads appropriate to the demand. Areas within cities and regions which had low levels of use and congestion would have low levels of investment in roads but their lower road prices would tend to attract development away from areas and regions with high levels of cost and congestion and therefore higher prices. It would be expected that the charges would be high enough to deter some people from using the roads.

XIV Public Transport

The most sophisticated road pricing and regulatory system cannot meet all the demand for individual access to the rich variety of activities and services available in the modern city by private transport. All modern cities must have a public transport system if only to ensure a measure of equity in access by the old, the poor, the young and the disabled to those activities and services. It would, of course, also be available to all citizens who wished to use it. The public transport system may consist of a number of modes: ferries, buses, taxis, trams and trains. The demand for access to some activities and services in some locations in the city may be large enough to be most sensibly met by a high capacity public transport service. In some cases the demand is great enough to warrant the construction of fixed rail services. It is clear though that we cannot have a fixed rail public transport service which enables all demand for travel between all destinations in the city to be met economically. The question then becomes: what mode of service best meets the demand for public transport in different parts of the city?

Before cars were widely owned, fixed rail public transport services gave cities the ability to grow yet concentrate economic and social activities while simultaneously enabling their citizens to have the opportunity to enjoy living at the lower density their higher living standards permitted. The train systems were essentially radial in character with little opportunity for circumferential movement. The development of trams (or what we now call *light rail)* and, later, buses further extended the catchment of the city enabling even more households to live at lower density than in the older, inner areas but were also essentially radial. As cars became more widely used even more households were able to live at lower density. The suburbanisation of Australian cities began when they were small single centred towns and when the radius of development was restricted by the distance people could walk or had horse transport, and was hastened by the adoption of the car. That is, the suburbanisation of Australian cities commenced very early in their growth, long before the development of fixed track public transport and the motor car and became characteristic of them. Davison makes this point compellingly in his forthcoming book (G Davison, pers comm October 1995). The road systems which developed in this suburbanisation were also radial and most of the investment in them further reinforced this structure.

Few cities now have public transport systems, road-based or fixed rail, which cover their costs of operation. Australian cities are no different in this respect. That is, they require subsidies to operate their public transport services. Although the subsidies are socially supported, that is, they are accepted by governments, recently moves have been made to increase fares to reduce the subsidies. Another feature of the subsidies is that they are inequitable in their incidence in the sense that the whole community pays for them but only a minority of the population has access to the services. The radially oriented fixed rail public transport systems not only provide services which best serve those whose journeys are to the city centre, they are also conveniently located for only a small proportion of the population. In some cities this outcome is repeated in the publicly funded bus public transport services. In Sydney, for example, less than half the population has reasonable access to the government bus services whereas the whole population pays the subsidy for their operation.

Unfortunately contemporary urban policy seems fixated on the introduction or re-introduction of fixed rail public transport into Australian cities. Such systems are focused on the *city centre* even though the centre is no longer the destination for most work, shopping, cultural and recreational travel.

A major justification often offered for further development of fixed rail public transport is the claim that such systems are less damaging to the environment because they consume less energy. Typically proponents show that the energy taken to move a person over a specified distance is lowest for trains, then trams, buses —and finally cars use the most. However, once the estimates are adjusted to take account of vehicle occupancy and the system operation costs for each, the differences are greatly reduced. Moreover, the comparisons do not acknowledge that the energy cost of travel, especially for cars, has fallen significantly over the past 20 years.

We can and should make a case for investment in and maintenance of public transport systems but the environmental considerations do not appear to favour fixed rail systems. Road based public transport appears to offer the possibility of an appropriate trade off between equity, flexibility and environmental stress.

XV Energy Production

Much of the debate over energy has focused on its consumption. Most energy is consumed in urban areas but if we are to be concerned about global warming we should also be concerned about the environmental impact of its production.

For the purpose of this discussion we will assume that the most significant sources in terms of their increase in stress on the environment are coal, which is mostly converted to electrical energy, gas which is mostly used for heating and petroleum products a high proportion of which are used for transport.

Although its consumption occurs largely in urban areas, electrical energy is usually produced at distant locations on or near the coal fields. The conversion of coal into electrical energy occurs at a relatively low level of efficiency: the process of winning the coal, burning it, conversion of water to steam, steam to mechanical energy and mechanical energy to electricity is very inefficient (25 to 35 per cent). More losses occur in transmitting the electricity from the point of generation to its point of use. The overall system has a very low level of efficiency (about 20 per cent) which in turn means that electricity generated in coal fired power stations is done only at significant cost in terms of environmental stress in the production of waste heat, CO_2, CO, NO_x, SO_2, fly ash, and so on.

Denser forms of urban development rely on greater consumption of electrical energy which is not only more expensive in money terms but because of the low efficiency in its production and distribution is more expensive in terms of total energy consumption and therefore in its contribution to greenhouse gas production.

Natural gas is now the most common form of energy-as-gas. The production of gas, or more correctly, the extraction of gas and its transportation to the point of consumption incurs little loss of energy and therefore results in little environmental stress. Its consumption, however, does produce greenhouse gases and the heat of consumption also leads to environmental stress.

The production of petroleum products involves the refining of those products from crude petroleum and results in significant energy loss which almost invariably occurs in or close to the major urban areas in which the products are consumed. This energy loss is in the form of heat and the products of combustion of unsaleable fractions, evaporation and spillage which add directly to the greenhouse effect.

The energy costs of fabricating the power plants to produce electricity, of the system of pipes to transport the natural gas to the city and to distribute it within the city and the drilling equipment, rigs, pipelines and refineries for petroleum products are essentially met in the city. Those to develop the mines on the coalfields, establishing the gas and oil fields are usually met some distance from the city. They, nonetheless, all result in environmental stress in the sense that they all increase the greenhouse effect.

The form and structure of urban areas has little to say to environmental stresses resulting from energy production. More efficiently structured cities and those in which the form of development encourages greater use of renewable energy sources can reduce the demand for energy and thus the stresses from its production but the greater effects are more likely to be from increased energy prices, including taxes, which lead to more efficient forms of energy production.

We should note, however, that as innovations in solar energy conversion to electrical energy become more economically efficient new possibilities in the design of buildings and in the structure of cities are opened. The new solar energy conversion systems for example reduce the need for housing and other forms of development to be connected to centrally powered distribution networks and offer the opportunity of developing uniform power webs. That is they offer the opportunity of efficient electrical energy supplies to low density forms of development.

XVI Privacy and Independence

Privacy is highly prized in Australian urban areas. Households go to great lengths to ensure that they achieve as much privacy as possible. Planning and housing regulations are built on the need to preserve privacy. Part of the attraction of the detached house lies in the fact that its separation from other dwellings gives households a high degree of privacy from their neighbours. The conventional lot allows a house to be set back from the street and gives households a high degree of visual and aural privacy. Typically, traditional residential developments afford households protection from being *overlooked* so that their outdoor spaces are also private. Many medium to high density developments including those built under the AMCORD Urban Code, sacrifice privacy, effectively forcing people to take refuge in the interiors of their dwellings or to be quiet for fear of being overheard. Those with even moderate hearing difficulties who play their radios or televisions loudly impose a burden on their neighbours. The closeness of dwellings means that in hot weather, when windows are opened privacy is virtually non existent.

Many medium density developments, high and low rise, are established under strata title legislation. That is, the owners of the separate dwelling *units* also have shares in and responsibility to a *body corporate* which has responsibility for the overall management and maintenance of the development. It can decide how frequently maintenance is carried out and by whom and it has the power to strike levies to pay for such maintenance. It can establish and enforce the rules governing the development including whether pets can be kept, washing hung out to dry, whether units can be sub-let and how the common areas are to be used. It is not uncommon for individual unit occupiers to feel that their privacy and independence is compromised by the activities and operations of the body corporate in their development. Although some of the rules may be petty, attempts by bodies corporate to achieve compliance with them can be significant sources of tension. In traditional housing these sources of friction are rarely evident.

Proponents of consolidation rarely consider the experience residents have with the difficulties of cooperative living arrangements.

XVII Amenity

The level of amenity of a development is a function of its convenience and of the open space and facilities available as well as the quality of landscaping and aspects of civic design. The convenience is a measure of its ease of access to a range of services. Developments in the postwar period were required to have various services such as schools, shops and open space available within a specified distance. Under current policy these standards have been revised downwards: schools are no longer provided as close to homes;

and less public open space is provided for active and passive recreation. The result is that, with the dwellings themselves also having less garden space, the developments are returning to a density of development which postwar planning was devised to alleviate. The *tighter* road and footpath space means there is less space for public tree planting to relieve the monotony of the poor quality architectural design of the dwellings or to clean the air. The smaller lots in the higher density subdivisions are usually too small to allow even medium sized trees to grow. In a word, the quality of amenity is lower.

In existing areas the policy of consolidation almost invariably leads to a loss of privacy and amenity. The loss of privacy occurs because the higher density housing inserted into existing developments often leads to overlooking and development of housing which can be looked into by passers by. The loss of amenity occurs because vistas are blocked and more households now make use of facilities which are often already under provided. Households in areas where dual occupancy occurs may find that their area which may have been detached housing occupied by a *normal* distribution of households is converted to one for a population of transient households which they may regard as a loss of their amenity or community coherence. Dual occupancy might work to the short term advantage of an individual household or developer but usually has significant restructuring effects on the amenity of the rest of that community.

It is very difficult to increase the level of privacy or to improve the level of amenity once an area is developed. If these factors are not taken into account in the initial design and development they are compromised for a long time. The protagonists of consolidation rarely point out that they can only achieve the *savings* they claim by significant reductions in privacy and amenity which are essentially collective attributes of a neighbourhood.

XVIII Summary

The torrent of expressions of concern about the need to focus on ecologically sustainable development raises serious questions about the way we develop and manage urban systems. The issue is, however, more complex and problematic than contemporary urban policy appears to recognise. A full accounting of the social and environmental consequences of the form and structure of our cities and the way they are serviced would suggest a change in policy over the directions which have been taken. At the very least this preliminary review suggests that the simplistic initiatives designed to produce *consolidation* are more likely to intensify environmental stresses rather than ameliorate them.

XIX Paradoxes

This discussion has shown that the pursuit of environmental concerns is not as simple as is suggested in current housing policy. Following the current facile propositions will in all probability make the situation worse.

We see that increasing housing density:

- actually decreases our capacity to cope with domestic wastes and our opportunities for recycling;
- reduces our capacity to harvest or otherwise cope with the rainfall on urban areas and reduce runoff;
- makes it harder for urban residents to produce much of their own food;
- increases air pollution because it reduces space for growth of trees and shrubs to purify the air and cool the urban area;
- reduces chances of growth of wood for fuel and reduces habitats for birds and other native fauna;
- increases congestion which increases accidents and energy losses.

We also see that the reduction in energy consumption in housing thought to be associated with increased dwelling density is more apparent than real and is more likely to be related to the numbers in each household.

The paradox is that even if we assume that increased density leads to reduced energy consumption and that this is *good* because it is an environmental benefit, it is offset by the environmental deterioration experienced in other parts or elements of the urban system.

Chapter 4

EFFICIENCY AND EQUITY OF POLICY MEASURE

Consolidation policy is implemented through a series of policies and programs initiated at Federal and State levels. The main elements of the policy are:

- Granny Flats and Dual Occupancy
- Green Street
- AMCORD Urban
- Building Better Cities.

I Granny Flats and Dual Occupancy

Following the flat construction *boom* of the early 1960s Sydney experienced the construction of a rash of illegal *granny flats* in the late 1960s and early 1970s. Local government councils sought powers to regularise the situation and to reassert their authority in the control of development. By 1980 the continued urban expansion and the perceived costs of services led the New South Wales Government to seek ways of slowing down what was regarded as excessive expansion of the fringe areas of Sydney. Local government was in a quandary: on the one hand they needed to regulate the situation but on the other the new State Regional Environment Plan No 1 (SREP 1), gazetted in 1980, amended Planning Scheme Ordinances requiring 26 local government authorities in the Sydney region to permit all attached dual occupancy developments with a floor space ratio of 0.5:1 on lots of 400 square metres and more, and to permit detached second dwellings on lots of 600 square metres, provided the height of the second dwelling did not exceed 3.6 metres. Local authorities could attach a condition for development consent requiring the owner to occupy one of the dwellings (there was a great degree of variation between councils in the application of this condition), the term *granny flats* being replaced in this period by the more neutral *dual occupancy*.

Although this SREP 1 directive was resisted by local authorities and criticised on equity grounds, the government promulgated the consolidation policy in 1981 and, under SREP 2, required a further nine local authorities to approve the dual occupancy proposals.

Local authorities campaigned against government initiatives to further reduce their discretion over development control in their areas during the mid-1980s. Although local authorities won some minor concessions, in 1987 the government introduced SREP 12 which greatly reduced local discretion by setting standard conditions for 43 local authorities in Sydney and removed the requirement which had restricted dual occupancy to owner occupiers, a condition which was difficult to enforce, and granted as-of-right development permission to owners of traditional house properties throughout the State. Under SREP 12 detached dwellings could be erected on lots of more than 600 square metres with a floor space ratio of 0.5:1 (with some exceptions such as North Sydney, Leichhardt, Marrickville and Randwick in which higher floor space ratios were allowed in accordance with their own plans). In those areas where flat developments were permitted the dwellings could be strata titled which meant that dwellings could be separately sold. Removal of the requirement that owners reside in one of the dwellings meant that commercial investors could develop and lease, and, in some zones, sell both dwellings. Although their powers have been weakened, many local authorities have continued to use all the openings available to them to oppose the *carte blanche* dual occupancy policy and have succeeded in winning some minor amendments. As all dual occupancy developments require development consent, local authorities are required to apply the *Environmental Planning and Assessment Act* 1979 (EPAA) under s 90 of which factors such as the impact of the proposed development on the environment, the social and economic effect on the locality, the character, bulk, shape and so on of the proposed development and its impact on the amenity of the neighbourhood may be taken into account. This has given local authorities some measure of control but they are under significant pressure from the State Government to allow dual occupancy applications. Neighbours have to be advised of all Development and Building Applications for dual occupancy but their only avenue of objection is through the courts and is restricted to *procedural* issues such as whether the local authority adequately considered privacy in granting development permission. A small number of local authorities on the fringe of Sydney able to demonstrate that dual occupancy is inappropriate for their area have been exempted from SREP 12 on environmental grounds.

At the same time as SREP 12 was introduced in 1987 the State Government gazetted State Environmental Planning Policy (SEPP) 25, which was designed to reduce housing costs by allowing the construction of single dwellings on small lots. SEPP 25 also sought to encourage innovation and diversification in subdivision, site plans and design through integrated housing development. Minimum lot sizes of 232 square metres, the historical minimum under the *Local Government Act* 1919 (NSW) (now reduced to 230 square metres) were permitted for single dwellings to encourage higher density while not permitting flat developments. Such developments were not to be subdivided until all dwellings in it were completed. This constraint impeded the financing of such developments and the restriction was removed when the SEPP was amended in 1988. The policy was reinforced by publication in 1988 of the Department of Environment and Planning's strategy document *Sydney Into Its Third Century,* which stressed the importance of a general increase in urban densities. The strategy proposed an increase in density in new areas from eight to ten lots per hectare and a doubling of the proportion of dwellings built as townhouses and flats.

The 1991 amendment of SEPP 25 followed a review of it and SREP 12 in 1988, which recommended that dual occupancy be allowed anywhere in the State where residential development was permitted and that the subdivision and issuing of separate title of lots on which dual occupancy developments occur be allowed. SEPP 25 as amended together with SREP 12 has placed local authorities increasingly at the mercy of developers thus further reducing their capacity to determine the kind and quality of development in their areas. The justification for the policy and associated administrative measures was that the increased density would lead to economies in infrastructure provision and lower housing costs but the Department of Planning and Environment produced no research evidence to support its contention. Nor has it produced any evidence that the policies have had those effects.

Local Councils could develop their own housing strategies and become exempt from SREP 12 and SEPP 25 although they were still subject to the general directions of State Government policy. Eleven Councils did so. Following the 1995 elections and change in government the right to subdivide dual occupancy developments was removed although the Ministerial decision did not affect the eleven Councils which had developed their own housing strategies.

The policy of allowing *granny flats* was introduced in Canberra in 1978. Proponents of granny flats were mindful of the negative reaction to the *six and twelve pack* developments of flats and home units of the early sixties in Sydney, so they proposed that households be allowed to construct a separate self-contained flat on blocks occupied by single family houses. The comfortable and attractive assumption was that this would enable families to return to some imagined halcyon past by creating conditions in which the extended family could flourish again by allowing elderly relatives to live with but independently of their families. There never were enough grannies to go around to justify the policy so the flats became general additions to the stock of rental housing. The sensible response would have been to allow small self-contained units to be built as part of a dwelling not allowing them to be subdividable and hence not separately saleable. The flats would have been readily reversible, if necessary, to meet the needs of later occupants of the enlarged dwelling. This would have met the objectives of being able to arrange accommodation for the extended family without the long-term undesirable irreversible effects which dual occupancy has had.

The reality that dual occupancy was an opportunity for speculative investment is confirmed by a survey in Sydney which found that 47 per cent of dual occupancy was undertaken by developers and 53 per cent by existing owners of whom only 15 per cent proposed to live in one of the residences. That is, 92 per cent of developments are for speculative development (*Urban Scrawl* 1994) which in the past has resulted in significant injury to the amenity of the areas where such development has occurred.

In the mid-1980s as-of-right dual occupancy development was permitted in Victoria (1985) and the Australian Capital Territory (1986). These initiatives were taken to clarify the situation which had developed in both jurisdictions by giving legal certainty to the developments which had occurred and to encourage yet more *consolidation*.

The argument was made that many traditional houses had gardens which were now too big for the houses' occupants and that it would be making efficient use of the land and services by allowing owners to build dwellings on this *unused space.* The policy gave everyone the right to build such a dwelling on their block if the block was larger than some minimum size. In Victoria the minimum lot size is 450 square metres and one of the dwellings must be less than 100 square metres and the maximum total site coverage is 60 per cent. It has led to a flood of applications for approval of proposals to build additional dwellings in the *backyards* of houses and for the extension and subdivision of existing houses. A key element of the policy was the change in the law which gave these dwellings separate titles: owners were allowed to strata title their property or sell the dwellings with community title.

In the older inner areas the provision of open space and recreation facilities is usually below standard. In Sydney for example an essential element of the County of Cumberland Planning Scheme—*Sydney's Great Experiment* (Winston 1957) was the creation of a fund to acquire property to provide open space in established areas to bring the areas up to standard. The inner areas were particularly poorly served with open space so the program was directed to acquiring sites and developing parks from *pocket handkerchief* size up to those large enough for organised sports. The Cumberland Planning Scheme did not identify sites in the inner area to be acquired for open space because it was believed that as sites were cleared for redevelopment the deficiency in open space could then be rectified. The inner areas did not achieve the target levels of provision on a per capita basis until the population fell and they never achieved it in terms of the proportion of the area devoted to open space. The Wran Labor Government established an Inner City Open Space Acquisition Program to start to redress the problem but the program was abandoned by the Greiner Government. It would be ironic if the consolidation policy succeeded in increasing population to levels where they would again be under-provided with open space.

Another paradox is that although the policy of consolidation was conceived as a way of increasing density in the inner areas it has actually had most effect in increasing density in the outer ring or peripheral areas of the city. This is the worst possible result because it reduces amenity with no improvement in efficiency. It is producing developments that are under provided with schools, open space and community facilities.

The *blanket*, as of right, dual occupancy policy, which could be applied anywhere and everywhere, has resulted in dual occupancy development in even the most inappropriate locations and has left all areas with the threat that the blight of consolidation could be visited on anyone if their neighbours, or some developer, decided that they wanted, for whatever reason, to develop their site to greater density.

II Mean Street Not Green Street

An integral component of the consolidation policy was the introduction of the Green Street program. Under this program communities were adjured to adopt new approaches to development in which dwellings were to have zero lot lining (meaning that dwellings could be built to the boundary of the land) to eliminate or greatly reduce the separation between dwellings; to be connected to one another either as terraces or semi detached houses; to have narrow streets, minimum pavement widths, reduced footpaths and *nature strips* with rollover kerbing which allowed vehicles to easily mount the nature strip to park or pass; and reduced setbacks. Research carried out under the Green Street Joint Venture into Housing Attitudes in Australia (1991: 7) found that "[T]he traditional detached house on the large block is still the most preferred housing form." The market research was nonetheless directed to finding ways to gain acceptance for consolidation. That is, the policy was not based on community aspirations, desires or expressed preferences but its proponents were determined to find ways of changing those preferences without necessarily engaging the community in a discussion of the desirability of doing so. Public relations programs were devised to *educate* the public to accept and even desire the kind of housing resulting from the policy. These were programs of manipulation and control rather than of participation.

Much has been made of the benefits which would flow from the Green Street program under which people were supposed to enjoy high quality urban development while sacrificing garden space.

Some of the early developments under this program have been for the upper end of the housing market and have produced large dwellings which met high design standards (*Development Now*, 1990-1995 various issues). Other developments under this program, including demonstration projects, have *become down at heel* very quickly. By and large they have also been redevelopments of small sites or amalgamations of sites in existing subdivisions and many of them have lacked conspicuous market success.

For the program to achieve the economies claimed for it large numbers of small dwellings in new subdivisions will have to be built for the lower end of the market. If the Canberra experience with Green Street developments is typical, apart from the *show piece* developments, the dwellings built under this program are not well designed and provide mean accommodation for low income households with children. There is little private outside space and little public open space, forcing children to use the street as their play space. In some developments the *dead end* streets are so narrow that service vehicles such as fire engines and garbage trucks can get access to dwellings only with difficulty. They are mean streets which recreate the conditions which modern housing standards were devised to overcome.

III AMCORD URBAN

The Australian Model Code for Residential Development: Guideline for Urban Housing (AMCORD URBAN 1992) was produced allegedly in response to *calls* from Premiers and Planning Ministers in 1991 for a higher density housing code. The code used to provide the administrative framework for the Green Street policy, is based on the premise that town houses, villa units and apartments are *urban* and implies that other forms of housing in urban areas such as detached houses are not. The term *urban* was introduced to overcome the alleged confusions over the meaning of medium density. (Such a definition of urban would not be acceptable to any statistical authority.) Here urban housing is defined to be housing on lots of less than 300 square metres with the expectation that the code would achieve densities in the range 25 to 100 dwellings per hectare.

Its proponents claim that this *urban housing* is an increasingly important form of cost-effective housing which offers:

- a range of sizes to suit different needs;
- good use of locations close to a wide range of facilities and public transport;
- a safe and secure environment;
- privacy;
- access to shared recreational facilities in some cases; and
- quality accommodation with minimal maintenance. (AMCORD Urban 1992: Overview)

The documents setting out the code do not explain how the form of housing actually does this and they contradict themselves. For example, although it is claimed that the higher density form of housing offers privacy, the documents actually say that:

> Some residents . . . may quite happily forego high levels of privacy in return for being able to live in an area that has valued attributes such as proximity to community facilities or public transport. (AMCORD Urban 1992: Overview)

They acknowledge that the higher density housing results in reduced privacy compared with conventional housing. An analysis of a project in Sydney reported that "It is apparent that residents are willing to accept a reduction in privacy where there is an improved sense of community." (*Development Now* 1994, 12:4). Although it acknowledged the loss of privacy the report did not show how the physical arrangement improved the sense of community nor how the willingness of residents to accept reduction in their privacy was expressed or assessed, the fact that the dwellings were occupied might simply reflect the lack of choice by the households concerned. Nor did the example show whether the occupants had better access to public transport.

Analysis of another project in Adelaide built under AMCORD and AMCORD Urban codes reported in *Development Now* (1994, 13: 5) that the road and parking space provision was inadequate and that: "[A]coustic privacy was a problem." The same report acknowledged that the dwellings and allotments were so small that the two car garages were often utilised for storage or recreation space. Inspection of the housing built in Canberra under this Code not only shows that the households have foregone privacy and open space but also that they do not have proximity to community facilities because there are none and the public transport is not especially good or close by either. A similar story can be told after inspection of such developments in Metropolitan Sydney but the documents ignore these facts.

While shared recreational facilities may be provided in a project as a substitute for the private open space in more traditional forms of development, they should not be allowed to be traded against the payment of developer contributions for public facilities in the general area. The provision of swimming pools and tennis courts and so on for the exclusive use of residents are private facilities for the benefit of households in that project and are provided by developers to aid the marketing of the project. They are not available to the general public and their provision may not reflect the perceived priorities of the general public. The provision of such private facilities actually increases the tendency for the development of *gated* developments which divide the community. Even when the open space internal to a development is public the local residents may not believe it is and may act to dissuade others from having access to it. That is, the policy leads to the development either of elite, exclusive ghettoes or areas of modern slums.

The objectives of the guidelines for urban housing include:

- achieving national objectives of social justice, micro economic reform and efficiency in land use;
- to encourage the provision of affordable urban housing for a changing population;
- to encourage quality urban design;
- to encourage a more consistent approach to State and local codes; and
- to provide flexibility in their adaptation and implementation at State and local levels (AMCORD Urban 1992: Overview).

We could hardly disagree that the pursuit of social justice is a laudable goal but how the Code or the consolidation policy is likely to contribute to it is unclear. It is more likely to work to the disadvantage of the lower income households because it leads to lower quality housing at lower standards of provision of open space and community facilities.

Micro-economic reform is meant to encourage more efficient use of resources and often involves reforming the working conditions of those engaged in government, commercial and industrial activities.

It is claimed that higher density housing results in more efficient use of infrastructure services and in that sense it meets the objectives of micro-economic reform but we have little evidence to support the assertion. The only evidence we have of more efficient use of resources from micro-economic reform in the construction of high density housing is the study by the AHIDC (1994a, 1994b) which recommends reduction in working conditions and job security for those unionised workers who work in the higher density sector of the house construction industry.

It is claimed that higher density housing leads to greater efficiency in land use but, as explained earlier, apart from the marginal reduction in the amount of land used for housing, the size of the city is little changed unless the reduction in residential land is accompanied by a significant reduction in open space for recreation, and reduction in land for public purposes and roads and footpaths. Limiting the size of the city increases the price of land so the efficiency may well be offset by a significant increase in price. The *efficiency* is also bought at a price paid in the form of a reduction in amenity, an increase in environmental stress, a reduction in adaptability of the housing, all of which are experienced largely by the lower income members of the community.

The objective of affordable housing is also laudable but all the research indicates that higher density housing actually costs more. The emphasis on the *changing population* is again unexplained. The population has always been changing. The objective implies that traditional housing is not or has not been affordable for the population but no evidence is presented to support the contention. Nor is any evidence advanced to show how the traditional form of housing fails or has failed to meet the changing needs of the community or of the individual households. Implicit in the notion that the stock of housing fails to meet the needs of the changing population is the proposition that households should change their dwellings when their household size changes but this objective contains no recognition of the costs of this approach to housing stock management, how it is beneficial, or of its consequences for community coherence/self-determination/autonomy.

The objective of encouraging quality urban design is one of those meaningless objectives used to *pad out* the list to make it look substantial. It implies that only higher density housing will always achieve higher *quality design*, yet few of the projects actually built indicate any understanding of what constitutes good design. Few of the lower income projects built to the guidelines are designed to take advantage of natural heating and cooling opportunities and few are well designed for access by service and delivery vehicles. Few are landscaped but most have a plenitude of paved areas and they rarely have any kind of pleasing aspect or outlook. Most have pocket handkerchief sized open spaces for clothes drying and are surrounded by high fences or walls which create an overpowering sense of enclosure. To the extent that they have any attractiveness it comes from their newness. Those built soon after the introduction of the Code already exhibit a *down at heel* air.

It is clear that some political leaders are exercised by issues of urban design. Comments are made about the poverty of design in Australian cities. References are made to *better design* in other cities and urban developments in earlier periods. Those who make the comments seem untroubled by the fact that most of the illustrations they give are of developments undertaken by dictators or autocratic rulers. They seem not to recognise that a major element in the unity of design and or materials employed in their favoured developments were the limited choices of materials and understanding of their behaviour as well as limited structural engineering capacities. Nowadays developers have virtually no limitations in their choice of materials nor are they limited by technology in the scale of developments they wish to undertake. When these facts are aligned with greater fragmentation in the ownership of urban land it is small wonder that there is little apparent unity in design. Moreover it is not clear that strengthening central control over design will improve it.

The objectives of encouraging consistency of approach to State and local codes and flexibility in their adaptation and implementation appear mutually exclusive. On the one hand they suggest that local authorities should be consistent with one another, a pressure which results in standards of the lowest common denominator, yet they also claim to provide for variation which would allow local government policies to reflect the different preferences of their residents. In the event, the way the codes are imposed on local authorities and the way citizens have had their rights of appeal reduced, suggest that the commitment to local flexibility, expression and autonomy is hollow.

IV Building Better Cities

At the Special Premiers' Conference in July 1991 the Commonwealth, States and Territories agreed to cooperate in a Building Better Cities Program, for the:

> Purpose of improving urban consolidation and the quality of urban life, in order to demonstrate at a practical level:
> - better planning and service delivery; and
> - coordination within and between the various levels of government.

By the time this was reflected in an Agreement with the States it had been translated to a Program whose objectives were to:

> Promote improvements in the efficiency, equity and sustainability of Australian cities, and to increase their capacity to meet the following objectives:
> - economic growth and micro-economic reform;
> - improved social justice;
> - institutional reform;
> - ecologically sustainable development; and
> - improved urban environments and more liveable cities. (Victorian Agreement 1991: 3)

The Agreement was to be in force to 30 June 1996 and to provide General Purpose Capital Assistance of up to $816 million. In (1994) the program underwnet a *facelift* and was subsequently described as the Better Cities Program.

Although there was an apparent softening of the commitment to consolidation between the Special Premiers' Conference and the Agreement with each State the program became one of the central elements in the consolidation policy. The range of projects funded under the program have been justified on a variety of grounds but how they meet the program's objectives is often hard to determine; it requires an elastic interpretation of the objectives. The program lacks focus and appears to have as its major benefit the fact that it gives States some additional funds with which they have been able to undertake a series of projects which have, and can have, no major effect on the decision-making process in respect of urban development. Many of the projects funded under the program or attributed to it were initiated before the program was conceived or would have proceeded without Commonwealth funds. In other cases the State and local governments concerned should have been required to undertake the projects without additional funding. In many cases the projects have been undertaken with little or no public involvement. In a number of cases the projects have led to gentrification which has not improved the social justice of those low income households who resided in the area before the project was undertaken. It is interesting that the brochures for the program for each State use the same illustrations and appeal to the same imagery. It is as though the authors of the program believe that the same solutions or the same built environments are appropriate for all Australian urban areas (BBC brochures nd).

The program is often described as a *demonstration* program but what is being demonstrated to whom is not clear. There seems little recognition in the design or implementation of the program of the chequered history of the large number of *demonstration* projects which have been undertaken internationally and in Australia by earlier State governments, and Federal governments to try to *educate* decision makers or the community in better ways of proceeding with urban planning or housing initiatives. How the various projects under the BBC program have led or will lead to a change in institutional arrangements or in the way decisions have been or are being made remains to be clarified. It is not clear for example what changes have been made in the institutional arrangements at State or Federal level which were conditional on projects under the program being funded.

Proponents of the BBC program claim that it involves collaboration and coordination between the three levels of government. A major difficulty with this claim is that simultaneously, State governments have reduced the power of local government to object to proposals which affect them. Over the same period the BBC program was introduced State governments have significantly weakened town and regional planning legislation, giving private interests greater weight in decision making and reducing the ability of community and *third party* interests to object to development proposals. That is, the collective consumption issues inevitably raised in considerations of the way cities grow and are operated are not addressed in the program.

Over the postwar period the relationship between governments and their bureaucracies has changed. Governments once largely confined themselves to policy issues and the bureaucracy administered the policies and programs in accordance with the legislation, regulations and instructions of Ministers. There was some separation of governments from their administration. Governments were thought to develop policy and programs, bureaucracies administered them. This was justified on the grounds that the administration was comprised of public servants who had permanent positions and gave independent, frank and fearless advice without favour to governments regardless of their political complexion. Significant elements of the administrative system were designed as statutory authorities to try to ensure that services, especially urban services, were delivered in accordance with sound economic principles and honest administration. Urban planning processes were established and city plans produced which were based on assumptions of detachment and professionalism.

State governments increasingly found these constraints unacceptable. Ministers sought and gained increasing control over the daily activities of statutory authorities and of their departments. Although planning was always a political process, in the sense that city plans were designed to express the priorities and preferences of the community, Ministers increasingly sought to politicise the daily administration of urban development. City plans became increasingly irrelevant as Ministers entered into the decision making and focused on short-term development proposals. A favoured device was to excise areas of the metropolitan area—such as Circular Quay, the Rocks and Darling Harbour in Sydney, Brisbane's and Melbourne's Southbanks—from the plans covering them. Plans themselves became less precise as planners attempted to respond to calls for greater flexibility and adaptability. The argument that metropolitan areas had to be *managed*, not planned, gained sway although how you could manage without a plan was never spelled out. In an important article discussing the connection between urban planning, policy and management, Neutze (1982) explored the limitations of the new fashion for *management* but his warnings seem not to have been heeded. Expertise and experience in an area was regarded as dangerous, evidence emerged that the expert had been *captured* by the clients, and *Managers* were appointed to head government departments and agencies replacing those with training, experience and expertise. The era of managerialism had arrived.

As Ministers increasingly sought to be involved in the minutiae of development control, they effectively became the managers with so-called *Chief Planners* or Departmental Heads being reduced in their power and significance. Metropolitan plans were effectively discarded. Governments adopted slogans such as "Doing more with less" to claim that the efficiencies of their policies and programs would produce more in spite of the cuts in revenue they introduced. The claimed efficiencies exceeded by substantial margins what was realistically achievable with the result that services were cut.

For similar reasons and simultaneously the relationship between Commonwealth Ministers and their departments changed and they also became more intimately involved in the daily administration of their portfolios.

This is the context in which the Building Better Cities program evolved. The program did not evolve from a sustained critique of urban issues and the problems confronting Australian cities. The program grew out of a short-term pragmatic desire to want to be seen to be doing *something* and to take advantage of an opportunity which arose because some resources had become available. The question which remains is: better cities for whom? Apart from the fact that the program is silent on these distributional issues it fails to show what kind of better planning is needed. Governments had for two generations accepted, in principle, that there was a need for better coordination between public and private investment but failed to achieve it. The new program fails to show how better coordination might now be achieved when all earlier attempts have failed. One of the unresolved paradoxes of urban development is that the very discipline and consistency in decision making, which a planning system implies must be accepted, is the source of its weakness. Planners have argued for high levels of coordination and have heard Ministers and developers agree that it is desirable, but they have had to cope with the frustration of seeing their arguments ignored each time particular proposals come before them. How were a few demonstration projects going to influence the realities of the political processes in urban decision making in a market economy? The mid-program report (BBC 1994) describes some projects which have some benefits in themselves and will, no doubt, lead to some *bits* of development which are of reasonable quality. Inclusion of most of the projects under the program's umbrella is no more than padding and none are the product of significant community demand, they are all *top down* initiatives and some, like the Pyrmont–Ultimo project, will actually create major problems for the operation of the city if they are half way successful in meeting their housing or employment objectives. The additional point which should be made in relation to Sydney is that it is inequitable to focus on central area investment when the major deficiencies in transport and community facilities faced by that city are in its outer areas to the west, southwest and south. Other projects like the Honeywell development in Newcastle do not appear to be based on a rigorous analysis of that city's present opportunities or prospects.

The mid-program report shifted the focus of the program from consolidation to planning, management and the need for infrastructure development. Although the understanding of Australia's urban history, which seemed to underlie the program's rationalisation, was seriously flawed (BBC 1994: iii), we can agree that there is a major role for the Commonwealth to play in addressing urban issues and in particular in overcoming the problems created by decades of neglect and under investment in infrastructure. There was a belated attempt, post hoc, to develop an analytical rationale for the Program. A major danger in recent development of urban policy lies in the way argument was made to *fold* housing responsibility into the BBC Program on the ground that the connection between housing, employment and transport is central to the development of better cities and that by placing investment in housing under the BBC Program those connections would be better made.

Another major problem with this type of *product* program is that most of the projects in them have long lead times and by the time they result in actual construction the Ministers and their advisers have moved on to another area of responsibility or retired from politics altogether. The projects may be seen by them as appropriate monuments to their energy and endeavours but they rarely lead to the changes in process which politicians claim as their rationale.

Table 4.1

Ownership Rates by Marital Status and Age Group 1982-1990

Age of Head of Household	1982	1986	1990
		Married Couples	
Under 25	30	32	27
25 - 29	61	59	56
30 - 34	74	73	72
35 - 44	82	82	83
45 - 64	87	88	87
Over 64	88	88	89
		Single Persons	
Under 25	7	9	10
25 - 29	24	26	27
30 - 34	33	38	40
35 - 44	51	55	53
45 - 64	68	64	67
Over 64	71	72	77
		All Households	
Under 25	20	18	16
25 - 29	49	48	45
30 - 34	65	64	63
35 - 44	76	76	75
45 - 64	82	82	80
Over 64	79	80	82

Source: Bourassa, S, Greig, A & Troy, P 1995, The limits of housing policy: home ownership in Australia; *Housing Studies*, 10(1): 83.

V Equity Effects

In a speech to the Third National Infrastructure Conference on 3 September 1990, Mr Howe, the then Minister for Community Services and Health, said that:

> It is clear that from environmental, economic and social justice perspectives, urban consolidation is a sound policy, *provided* [emphasis added] the rising costs of housing and the reduced access of lower income groups to traditional Australian housing styles which will accompany such a policy can also be addressed. (Howe,1990: 9)

We can ignore the fact that Howe provided no supporting evidence for his assertion about the soundness of his policy but note that in adding this proviso Howe revealed some concern for the central claims of the policy, a concern which seems subsequently to have melted in spite of the mounting evidence that the environmental and economic rationalisations for the policy were and are contentious and problematic. In acknowledging that consolidation increased housing costs and reduced access to the traditional housing for the lower income groups, Howe was acknowledging that the policy was regressive. These equity issues have not been addressed: housing costs have not fallen. Data in 1991 on home ownership rates suggests that home ownership among the young continues to fall, although young single households appear to go against the trend (Table 4.1). Since then there have been rises and falls in affordability with changing interest rates. Moreover, waiting lists for public housing continue to grow, reaching 233,370 by 1994 (Table 4.2) and the numbers of homeless appear to have increased (Australian Institute of Health and Welfare 1995). This deterioration in the housing situation is unlikely to have followed solely or even significantly from the consolidation policy although that policy must have contributed. It is more a result of persistent high levels of unemployment.

The housing policies pursued in the postwar period together with the continued attendant suburbanisation of the city was one of the ways in which the lower income members of Australian society obtained a greater share in its wealth (Stretton 1987). The policies were part of the commitment to egalitarian principles. They enabled households to progressively increase their equity in housing including their use of *sweat equity* or self-help opportunities.

While Kemeny challenged this view in his *Great Australian Nightmare* (1983) arguing that owner occupation had fostered individual houses and encouraged *sprawl*, Hayward (1986) pointed to the flaws in his argument: that the form of housing together with home ownership policies enabled households, especially lower income households, to have greater control over their situation, to control their costs and to enjoy the stability and benefits which grew out of their development of a sense community. Lower income households now have less opportunity to control their housing conditions or costs and consolidation will reduce their opportunities still further.

Table 4.2

Public Housing Wait Lists by State 1994

State	Public Housing Dwelling Units	Households on Wait List
WA	35,000	14,350
NSW	127,000	84,000
ACT	12,500	6500
QLD	41,000	24,500
SA	63,000	43,520
TAS	14,200	5000
NT	9000	8000
VIC	66,000	47,500

Source: National Shelter Issues paper 2, *Public Housing in Australia: Issues and Directions for Change, 1994.*

The physical environment is not the only or even the most important factor affecting equity or the development of a sense of community. Nevertheless the recent adoption of consolidation policies runs counter to the pursuit of equity because it is predicated on notions of encouraging/forcing households into smaller dwellings with less space and lower levels of amenity. The policy also requires households to move as they grow then fall in size, making it more difficult to develop a sense of community.

Proponents of consolidation policies point to the present apparent *success* of the policy in the sense that dwellings built under it appear to be meeting a demand. Because the market is *clearing*, proponents argue it is popular although we are also told that there is evidence of over supply of the medium and higher density inner city housing. A more important point, however, is that the supply is being managed to ensure this *success*. While the population of the city continues to increase there will be a continuing demand for housing and if the supply is managed so that the majority of dwellings provided are medium density they will be taken up. This will be the case especially where governments contrive to produce a price advantage in favour of the higher density forms of housing because they believe (wrongly and without evidence) that its long-term environmental costs are lower.

Much of the argument for consolidation policies and programs has rested on simple minded physical determinism and a narrowly conceived and erroneous economism. Proponents have painted and dwelt on felicitous imagery of social interaction resulting from high density *urban* living and a vibrant *street life*. They appeal to some halcyon imagery of the past. They have rarely considered the ugly realities of the street life of the past or the reasons why it disappeared (Brown-May 1995).

The narrow economism bound up in the arguments that higher density housing reduces costs does not make clear that these alleged cost savings come from a reduction in standards. Shelter, like food, is a basic need. People know that when policy makers talk about cheaper food costs they invariably mean lower quality food lines. People also understand that cheaper housing means lower quality accommodation.

But the effect of the policy on family life is rarely considered. This writer argues that physical determinism should not be allowed to dominate policy nor should the physical conditions in which households live be ignored. The consequences for family life of reducing the size of dwellings, the garden space around them and the public open space nearby has not been explored. The assumption of consolidation policy is that there are no *downsides* to the policy.

The pressures households are subjected to as their living space is reduced, the way their options for activities are limited and the way households are limited in their capacity to respond to the changing needs of their extended families are not considered. The tensions in a family can be exacerbated because the dwellings and their gardens are too small for household members to *get away from one another* and may be destructive to the family. One of the benefits of larger dwellings is that household members have been able to engage in activities without irritating one another—teenagers who want to listen to heavy rock have been able to without intolerably annoying others; those who sought a quiet corner to read in while others watched TV have been able to do so. Outdoor space has allowed households a variety of outdoor activities in privacy and it has allowed individual members the space and flexibility to pursue their separate interests. In the past the garden space has enabled households to grow some of their own food, especially in periods of adversity. That option is removed when garden space is reduced. The pressures on household members to constrain their activities in the home brought about by inadequate space inside and outside the dwelling may surface as aberrant or antisocial behaviour in public.

The suite of urban policies, including consolidation, for all their grand titles, may be seen as part of the response of the Australian government to the fashionable ideology of *globalisation*. The present urban policies are an integral part of the attempts to reduce protectionism. The policies are the working out of the push to reduce regulation and to reduce standards to make the economy more *efficient* and *competitive*. The only members of society in no position to resist these initiatives are those on low incomes.

Chapter 5

DEMOCRACY, PARTICIPATION AND CITIZENSHIP

The formulation of public policy is not a simple clean process. The logics followed may not correlate well with the logics of science, economics or political and social theory. Moreover, public policy analysis is not an exact science. We note too that debates on public policy are often built on misuse or misinterpretations of statistical data, myths, fallacious or mutually exclusive propositions and unresolved paradoxes. In a few cases the debate on a particular area will embrace all these flaws.

Housing policy and urban policy are separate but closely related issues. In recent debates insufficient attention has been paid to the separate aspects of the two issues. Conflation of them has resulted in serious confusion.

One of the models of policy formulation and implementation commonly used to describe the public policy process in democracies like Australia is that the process is a cycle. It is assumed that the community in some way reveals a set of desires which are articulated through the political process into policies and programs which are supported through the electoral process by the public. The government then translates these policies or programs into instructions to its administration which then has the responsibility for implementation. The public then responds to the incentives or has to comply with the resulting rules and regulations. The model assumes that if enough of the public dislikes the policy it will transmit this feeling to the political parties which will then adjust their policies accordingly. On the other hand if the policies meet with the approval of the public, governments will be encouraged to persist with them. That is, in this model, policy is formulated in a bottom up way with the political parties responding to the community and providing focus for it.

Another model assumes that policy is established in a top down approach under which the government enunciates policy which the administration implements and which the public complies with. The public has little opportunity to express its views although it does have the right to reject the entire government at an election. This approach implies a high degree of paternalism on the part of the government and its administration.

Neither model adequately represents the political process especially in situations where more than one policy issue is at stake. The limitations are the more evident when a policy issue is perceived to have relevance for only a small proportion of the population at any given time or only indirectly bears on the lives of the majority. The limitations become even more obvious when outcomes of policies may have long-term effects or be expensive to ameliorate. Many urban policy issues appear to have these characteristics. Individual incremental development decisions are not seen as having any immediate impact on most people yet once the decisions are made, particularly those which affect dwelling construction, subdivision patterns and layout, the effects persist for a long time. For this reason it is important that urban policy options, especially those designed to effect major changes to the form and structure of the city, are properly researched and widely discussed in the community before a policy is adopted.

What is needed is an amalgamation of the two policy formulation models. In urban policy fields we can imagine situations where initiatives or policy discussions start, more or less simultaneously, at both the top and at the bottom and when they intersect we develop strong levels of commitment. This is not the character of contemporary urban policy initiatives in Australia, particularly the consolidation policy.

Another interesting feature of the consolidation policy is that, although it was initiated at the State level, much of the recent initiative for it comes from the Commonwealth level. Although the Commonwealth has limited constitutional responsibilities in housing and urban development, it has chosen to buy into the issue and take a leading role. It has done so as an exercise in top down articulation of policy with no claim that it is responding to community expressions of concern and no effort to engage the community in a debate over its efficacy. Even in the area where it has the most obvious responsibility for urban issues, the Australian Capital Territory, it has eschewed the opportunity to engage the community in discussing policy options. The approach by most governments, but especially the Commonwealth, to the introduction and implementation of the policy has been manipulative and authoritarian, brooking no disagreement.

For all the Commonwealth might claim that it has simply responded to a call from the States for involvement it has vigorously set the agenda and provided the staff and other resources to develop and implement the policy. Because it has such an indirect responsibility in this field the Commonwealth has more reason than the States for ensuring that any policy initiative in housing and urban development is soundly based. Although it was aware that the policy was highly contentious and had little research underpinning, the Commonwealth chose to adopt consolidation as the major way of tackling what it perceived to be an emerging set of issues. The States were no less determined to pursue consolidation as a panacea for the imagined infrastructure funding crisis despite the lack of research or public discussion of the issues.

It is tempting to describe the current suite of urban policy initiatives in terms of the dogmatic application of ideology but this would be seriously misleading. Some aspects of the consolidation policy imply a right agenda given that central to it is an argument for greater reliance on the market and the breaking down of planning and regulation. Other aspects of its implementation reveal an authoritarian, manipulative streak which is anti-democratic. Although in New South Wales its origins lay with a Labor government, subsequent Coalition governments have pursued consolidation policy, including dual occupancy, with at least equal enthusiasm. Opposition to the policy has come from Labor and Liberal councils to both Labor and Liberal governments so it is difficult to ascribe a simple ideological explanation to the actions of those who oppose it. The New South Wales 1995 State election was contested by the Stop Dual Occupancy Party and a number of the candidates, especially Labor, made much of their opposition to the policy in their campaigns. We should not conclude that the issue was central to the Labor victory but it was a significant background concern for many who felt their environment was under threat. They will not be consoled to see that the Carr Government has vigorously espoused similar compact city policies as its predecessors and with similar disregard for the views of residents.

Although the impetus for the consolidation policy at the Commonwealth level comes from some of the nominal left elements of the Federal Government, its essentially inegalitarian outcomes suggest that it can not fairly be described as left in its ideological origins.

But the question remains: why would a government pursue a policy for which there is little research backing, which runs counter to popular attitudes and mores and which is so inequitable? Part of the answer may be found in the desire of politicians to build their own monuments, to leave something point outable as their mark on society. There can be little doubt that this desire for personal aggrandisement infects the consideration of the issues at both levels of government. We note too, in passing, that politicians are not alone in the desire to leave their own monuments—bureaucrats seem to suffer similarly. Part may reflect an attitude like that of religious fundamentalists who are confident of their knowledge that they know what is best and, given that they have been blessed with power and resources, are determined to change things whether we like it or not. Part of the answer also lies in the managerialism which has destroyed expertise in the planning and servicing authorities.

Another part of the answer lies in the way new ideas gain currency in a society which has a politics of personalities and does not foster public debate on issues. The combative and oppositional nature of government ensures that policy formulation is rarely research or critique based. The consultation process governments employ is more manipulative than consultative, more concerned with what Dear calls the "[M]echanics of persuasion" (Dear 1989: 449) than with trying to develop a shared identification of the problems and understanding or even a consensus about what policies or programs should be adopted to solve them. Urban issues are always complex. The complexity often generates dilemmas for politicians and decision makers who search for solutions which they can explain to the public. In this situation the attraction of the simple solution can be overwhelming, partly because of a misperception that the public cannot understand complex issues. The problem is that the simple solution is almost always wrong. The urban problems which politicians faced in the early 1980s were massive and complex and the elegant simplicity of the consolidation policy promised a way out of their dilemmas. The lack of a research-based critique, a confused and limited understanding of environmental stress in urban areas and little understanding by the politicians and their advisers of the strength of views held by people about their environment led to the kind of popular resistance now being observed. A more sensitive response would have been to explore with the public whether alternative ways of solving some of the infrastructure funding issues could have been found and whether issues of environmental stress could have been more sensibly resolved.

A strong case can be made for Commonwealth engagement in housing and urban issues but how the issues are selected and approached is a matter of central concern.

In setting out to change the form and structure of the Australian city the policy of consolidation is designed to undermine the town planning policies and development control practices of the postwar period. It sets aside the consultative processes which have been slowly developed and which have acknowledged that individual households and the community as a whole have legitimate interests in commenting on and defending their environment. It is important to remember that the policy developed in a period when there were major moves towards deregulation in a wide range of public policy areas.

Developers and entrepreneurs have relentlessly pursued the argument that the regulations covering both housing and development control were too tight, that they stifled initiative and discouraged investment. Little evidence supports either of these propositions but they have nonetheless gained a currency which is now influential in policy debates.

The point has often been made that one of the strengths of local government is that it enables local communities to establish their own standards and to determine the kind and quality of development they wish to encourage in their areas. Apart from being an important commitment to notions of democracy and participation, this independence also has the virtue of encouraging diversity. Periodically this independence has, however, been seen as a hindrance to efficient development, raising the perpetual dilemma of the tension between efficiency and participation or democracy.

What is meant by efficiency is rarely spelled out. Ministers usually use the term to mean efficiency in some long-term, operational sense: the efficiency of operation of the city as a whole or the engineering efficiency of the urban services such as water supply, sewerage and drainage, public transport or the road system. Developers and critics of the system on the other hand usually refer to the short-term economic or financial efficiency of particular projects or patterns of development.

The tension between efficiency and democracy is inherent in any system of planning and development control. The democratic process must attempt to balance out the long-term interests of the community, including considerations of engineering efficiency, with those of private individuals. The process of consultation this usually entails is necessarily slow. Pressures by private individuals and corporations to depart from accepted standards and also to speed up the consideration of development applications, especially by removing or reducing the rights of residents or members of the community to express their views, is designed to subvert the planning and development control processes which protect community interests. That is, the pressure to allow market forces to dominate the development process would make public planning impossible and is inimical to community interests and to the democratic process.

The lack of national standards has been seen by some developers and politicians as leading to confusion and increased cost as development in one local government area spilled over into another adjoining it. There clearly are some areas where national standards are necessary: it makes no sense to have a variety of standards relating to plumbing or electrical fittings because the laws of hydraulics or electrical engineering are the same wherever you are and safety requirements do not vary. We cannot make the same arguments with equal force in areas of policy in which community perceptions about the urban environment are significant. While we can respond to an economic argument for standard plumbing and electrical fittings it is not clear that in most cases there is a need for other aspects of urban development to be standardised. In winning the argument for national standards the proponents of regulatory reform weakened the general case for regulations and undermined the case for local discretion.

The experience of local governments, especially in Sydney and to a lesser extent in Melbourne, in earlier periods of higher density development resulted in extensive areas of low amenity and poor quality housing with poor quality and under provision of community facilities. This experience led local governments to be wary of all requests for permission to develop to higher densities unless the development proposals were to high standards and included appropriate facilities. Local governments generally were determined to avoid a repetition of the excesses of Waverley, Randwick and Canterbury in Sydney and St Kilda in Melbourne. In addition to the demographic, infrastructure and environmental arguments for it, the consolidation policy was conceived as a way of breaking down this reluctance by the local authorities to countenance a reduction in their urban amenity.

Residents and local authorities who opposed consolidation have been described pejoratively as NIMBY's, people who said "Not In My Backyard!" The implication being that they supported the general thrust of the policy prescription but were too selfish to share the burden of its implementation or accept its implicit constraints. The epithet was picked up and turned on its head by those who oppose dual occupancy in Sydney and who fought against the invitations to Sydney residents to sell their backyards.

An alternative construction is that these people and their community institutions do not support the general policy. They are very concerned because they feel that the policy was ill conceived and under-researched and would more likely be detrimental to both their individual interests and those of the community generally. Moreover, they had not been given an opportunity to engage in the debates over the policy. The policy of consolidation came from a top down approach to policy formulation. It illustrates the main points made by Self in *Government by the Market* (1993).

Consolidation policy is based on the assumption that market determined outcomes will be efficient, equitable and appropriate. The community opposition to it which drew the NIMBY epithet could be interpreted as a community rejection of the notion of the benevolence of market-determined urban development and a rejection of pressures for consolidation. Wherever members of a community have a strong interest in its amenity we can expect opposition to policies or proposals which threaten that sense of community. To some extent NIMBY reactions may be intensified when governments say they are trying to develop a sense of community and to give people more choice. In locations where people have had their right to object seriously curtailed they might be more likely to resist consolidation initiatives.

Having failed to gain community acceptance of the policy, governments have resorted to a variety of stratagems. The Commonwealth has funded a series of education campaigns which are little more than propaganda and included subsidising ABC and SBS television programs, ABC radio programs and a wide variety of publications. It has also sponsored international experts who have toured the country lecturing and proselytising on the benefits of high density development but with no understanding of Australian urban history, its mores or its political and institutional structures. The Commonwealth has invested in projects designed to demonstrate the alleged benefits of the policy. State governments have more actively intervened to reduce the powers of citizens and their local governments to oppose or delay applications for permission to develop or redevelop at higher densities. They have ignored or over-ridden expression of community attitudes. We could ask: if the benefits of the policy are as manifest as its proponents claim, why have governments had to resort to *force majeur* to impose it on local government authorities? Why have citizens had their rights of objection reduced or eliminated?

For the reasons discussed above, the cities, especially the larger State capitals, have responded to the changing aspirations and behaviour of their residents. The adoption of a variety of technological innovations by residents, organisations and firms has led to Australian cities developing as multi-centred urban spaces. They have ceased to operate as single centred entities.

At its heart the effect of the policy of consolidation is to defend and further entrench central city interests. It fails to recognise the multi-centred functioning of the existing cities. The policy relies on the alleged benefits of a highly centralised fixed rail public transport system without acknowledging to whom the benefits accrue at whose cost.

Because the rich can always obtain as much space as they want and can travel freely about the city, the consolidation policy is effectively targeted at the lower income groups. Rather than increase choice for those with least resources the policy has the effect of reducing it. The rich are also better able to migrate to other centres and use the protection of convenants and other legal devices. The only groups which have to endure the reduction in living space and housing standards are those on the lowest incomes.

One of the consequences of the introduction of tight planning and development controls is an increase in land prices. The consolidation policy presupposes even greater limitations being placed on the supply of urban land. This will lead to even greater inflation in land prices and, ultimately housing prices. In none of the current consolidation programs or policies is this addressed yet as Evans (1988) points out, in England where there is a strong determination to preserve the countryside and to consolidate urban development, the ratio of urban to rural land price is very high. His solution is to reduce planning and development control to let the market increase supply and reduce prices. This writer does not endorse such a recommendation but Evans raises a legitimate consideration which has so far been ignored in the contemporary discussion of housing and urban policy in Australia, although Neutze raised the issue 20 years ago (Neutze 1975).

The paradox is interesting because, as we have discussed, some part of the argument for increased housing choice comes from the argument for deregulation. That is, consolidation is largely about loosening development controls, and allowing redevelopment at higher density or new development at higher density on the fringe. However, achievement of the objectives of the consolidation policy can only be through the imposition of tighter development control regulations in the sense that local community options are constrained by State government, by the direction of government investment in housing and infrastructure and/or by setting excessively high costs for urban services in new areas. The net effect of which will be to reduce choice.

One of the difficulties of critics of the policy is that it is extremely difficult for them to obtain access to information about the costs of urban services or to require that the information is made available on comparable bases. Political proponents of the policy are understandably loath to open the issue for genuine debate. Consideration of the policy is also affected by the traditional concerns in exploring many urban policy issues: those adversely affected by the policy may be weak, unorganised and have only a general public interest whereas those who stand to gain or who are directly involved in the policy's formulation have much to gain or lose, are strong and highly organised and have direct access to political power.

The proponents of consolidation discuss the policy as though its implementation will automatically lead to improved design and higher standard development. The actual experience with the policy suggests that consolidation policies lead to the replacement of single houses by the notorious six or twelve pack walk up flats or units which have minimal provision of facilities and are frequently on blocks which have little free space other than car parking (if they are lucky) and the site is usually concreted over. The reason we have seen strong community resistance to the policy lies in this experience. Regardless of the high claims made for it; householders and their local governments know that the policy leads in most actual cases to a loss of amenity.

In spite of the massive campaign mounted by governments to convince households of the wisdom of the consolidation policy and its imposition on communities, strong resistance to it has emerged. From the first consolidation initiatives in New South Wales local authorities and individuals opposed State government policies. In response, the State Government became even more authoritarian introducing changes through SREPs and SEPPs which progressively reduced local autonomy and choice. In New South Wales increasing numbers of local authorities have sought exemptions from the dual occupancy provisions of SEPP 25, even rural authorities such as Ballina have obtained Ministerial approval to an LEP which exempts new housing estates from dual occupancy provisions. Industry lobby groups such as the Housing Industry Association (HIA) have opposed these exemptions thus providing some evidence of who stands to gain most from the policy. Local councils are also increasingly listening to the objections of residents and refusing development permission for medium density redevelopment proposals on the grounds that they are inconsistent with and would injuriously affect the amenity of the existing development. The New South Wales Land and Environment Court has supported councils in cases taken to it on appeal by developers. The role of the courts in these issues can be important but it is more likely that this type of opposition will be employed in the higher income areas of the city with the result that the medium density housing will increasingly be concentrated in the lower income areas.

We are now witnessing increasing resistance to these policies as more people become exposed to their realities. In the 1994 Brisbane City Council elections strong opposition was expressed to the replacement of traditional housing by dwellings built under the consolidation guidelines and described as "dogboxes" and "sardine city" (vide BCC). Newspapers such as the *Sunday Age* (13 March 1994) and *Canberra Times* (25 March 1994) are carrying news items recording the mounting community opposition to consolidation along with stories supporting the policy (*CT* 25 March 1994).

Because opposition to consolidation policies in Melbourne threatened to become politically significant the Victorian Government in 1994 established a review of VICCODE 2. The panel reported in December 1994. Its main recommendations supported consolidation policy but sought to ameliorate its most contentious effects by encouraging medium density housing in the newly developing fringe areas, by allowing it in established areas where it could enhance and maintain their diversity and where local councils had developed a plan for their areas which included a vision of how they wanted their areas to develop. The panel recommended that beyond a radius of seven kilometres the permissible density for medium density housing in existing areas should be reduced but within that radius or on the larger sites densities in excess of 1:200 could be permitted. In March 1995 the government endorsed the main recommendations giving local councils more discretion over the protection of the character of their areas in the hope that consolidation projects would be better designed (the *Age* 1 March 1995).

In the Australian Capital Territory widespread opposition to dual occupancy and medium density housing led to the government commissioning a report from RB Lansdown designed to reduce the saliency of the issue. The report published in November 1994 conceded most of the arguments of the critics of the consolidation policy but the prevarication and lukewarm response of the government to the compromise proposed served simply to anger and further alienate the various local resident and environment groups and those concerned about the development of the city. The loss by Labor of the Australian Capital Territory elections in March 1995 arose in large measure because of widespread dissatisfaction and anxiety caused by its vigorous pursuit of consolidation policies and the consequent loss of amenity. The new government has not confirmed the compromise interim policy announced by the Labor government which means that the residents of Canberra remain subject to a high level of uncertainty about dual occupancy and medium density housing being visited on them.

In New South Wales the Department of Planning's response was to produce a Design Solution Manual to show how to produce better higher density housing. This has not satisfied local authorities like Concord which has threatened to refuse all dual occupancy and subdivision applications (*SMH* 20 March 1995), Sutherland which wants all dual occupancy banned, Mosman which wants exemption from the dual occupancy policy on the grounds that it degrades the environment (the *Age* 2 March 1995) and the other four north shore councils, Lane Cove, Willoughby, Hunter's Hill and Ku-ring-gai, which have sought exemptions and resisted consolidation policies especially that of dual occupancy.

The opposition of residents and their councils have forced major modifications to consolidation policy, especially to dual occupancy. It is clear however that significant areas of the major cities have suffered changes to their character that have reduced their amenity.

Much of the concern expressed by individuals and their local councils is that consolidation policies lead to a degradation of their environment and their amenity is reduced. They often also express the fear that their property values will fall. A preliminary study of the impact of medium density housing on adjacent property values in Adelaide came to the conclusion that "[T]he majority of developments assessed in the study increased or had no effect on the value of adjacent properties"(Babbage 1993: 31). Although the sample was small it acknowledged that some new developments did have an adverse effect on property values. Those developments which were poorly planned and unsympathetic to the existing development or which injuriously affected the privacy of the existing dwellings were most likely to reduce property values. Some real estate authorities acknowledge that consolidation policies including dual occupancy can have this effect in the better suburbs (the *Sydney Weekly* 21 March 1995). That is, research evidence and the opinion of experts in the property market indicates that residents' fears of adverse effects of consolidation policy on the value of their property are well founded.

Although consolidation has been a central element in the Commonwealth's urban and regional development policy initiatives we cannot conclude the consideration of them without discussing some of the other initiatives.

In New South Wales, Victoria, Queensland and the Australian Capital Territory all governments have responded to opponents of their consolidation policy with statements to the effect that they have no need to worry because the quality of design of the medium density housing would be so high it would enhance rather than detract from the amenity of areas. In some cases they have developed demonstration projects to show the superior quality environments which can result from the policy. By and large the ugly realities of the commercialism or bottom line development which has driven most medium density housing, including dual occupancy, built under the policy has meant that the promises of governments on behalf of developers have not been kept by the developers, whereas the fears of residents and their councils have been confirmed in concrete.

But the design issue has not disappeared. There are some, like the former Prime Minister Paul Keating who had a well-documented interest in matters urban, who believe that many of the city's problems can be solved simply by better design.

The word design is full of ambiguities. For many it is interpreted to relate to the aesthetics of developments, to the scale of a project relative to its surroundings and to the subtleties of detail which reveal how it integrates with or is sensitive to the existing environment, built or natural. It is essentially understood to refer to small scale elements of the city, a building, a small group of buildings or small area of the city such as a park or square. This is the divide between urban or civic design and town or urban planning. The distinction is sometimes difficult to draw but traditionally we have been able to do so in an acceptable, workable compromise. In the debate over urban issues those which are more affected by consideration of aesthetics and amenity, where architects and landscape architects are thought to have most to offer, are most likely to be seen as issues of design. Those which relate to questions of equity and efficiency, to structure, operation and administration of the city and its systems and to the environmental impacts of development, where town planners, economists, engineers, geographers and political scientists are thought to have most to offer in identifying problems, analysing them and setting out development options are most likely to be seen as issues of urban or town planning.

The Task Force on Urban Design in Australia established by the former Prime Minister has served to confuse the issue and cloud the debate over urban policy.

In its report the Task Force focused on three aims:

- to generate debate about the role of good design in providing livable, equitable and sustainable places to live and work;
- to identify practical and cost effective changes in industry, government and education across Australia;
- to suggest specific ways in which the Commonwealth can act to encourage good urban design. (Prime Minister's Urban Design Task Force 1994: 3)

In doing so it claimed a territory much larger than was traditional for design issues. The report also revealed a high degree of confusion and lack of understanding of urban issues confronting Australian cities.

The design gloss on the consolidation policy should be seen as another example of an elite group, out of touch with suburban Australia, attempting again to impose its views on the majority.

Chapter 6

AN ALTERNATIVE URBAN POLICY

A major problem with the *efficiency-based* approach to housing policy is that the solutions to problems, imagined or real, are *over determined*: they are too tight and allow little flexibility, freedom, or capacity to respond to changes in fashions, the transitions in the life courses of households and in the way we accommodate to changes in our consideration of environmental factors.

Underlying much of the concern over housing and related issues is a stated concern for social justice and the distributional outcomes of the way our cities are developed and operate. This is an important concern but it is not clear that current policies designed to improve narrowly defined *efficiency* in the use of the housing stock, or to change the form of the city by increasing its density will in any way serve that end.

The origin of the consolidation policy in a stated concern for the cost of urban services was based on a simple physical determinism which assumed that by increasing density the costs of services would be reduced. The policy took no account of the effects of increasing income on demand for them. It was assumed that if the residential areas were made smaller there would be a reduced demand for infrastructure investment. This proved to be illusory. The argument also failed to recognise the full effect of rising concern for the environment in the cost of services. It is unlikely that policies based on a simple physical determinism —in which the physical form of development is assumed to be the determinant of behaviour—and simplistic economism can long be sustained against economic and socio-political pressures.

The *environmental* case for consolidation has been reduced to a narrow and misleading concern for energy consumption. Supporters of this argument have argued for a compact city on the ground that such a city will reduce travel and therefore energy consumption. They have argued that jobs should be closer to homes: that housing and work places should be mixed together so that people will be able to find employment close to where they live and, further, that they will be able to satisfy their social and cultural needs close to home. The medieval city had these features: people lived over their workshops and found their pleasures close by, their horizons and understandings were similarly circumscribed. Is this the ideal proponents of consolidation work towards?

The proponents of the compact city with its mixed uses forget their own urban history. A major reason for the separation of homes from places of work was the injurious effect on people's health of many industries and workplaces. Another was the lower level of amenity mixed development offered. There is little evidence that modern factory managers are more prepared to voluntarily comply with noise, smell, effluent or air quality standards designed to protect the health of residents, especially children. Nor do they appear to be overly concerned about the effect of their factories on the level of amenity. The need for factories and warehouses to take delivery of or dispatch large loads means that in areas of mixed development, residents, but especially children, are put at greater risk of road accidents. Mixed development also places residents at greater risk of industrial accidents such as chemical spills, explosions and accidental release of toxic gases.

One problem with the *mixed use* strategy is that even if the initial users of a factory site or warehouse carry out their activities in harmony with residents there can be no guarantee that subsequent users, even those in the same land use category will do so. Once built the pressure would always be on local authorities to permit activities which complied with the use category for the site.

Another way of viewing the proposals for consolidation or *compact cities* is to see it as a new attempt to implement the arguments of Jane Jacobs, who sang the praises of high density living (Jacobs 1961). For a brief moment her arguments to create her romantic interpretation of the lifestyle she observed on the streets of New York held some sway. Her arguments were rebutted in Australia by Hugh Stretton (1970: 4):

> The Australian preference for family life in private houses and gardens is probably intelligent. Instead of despising the suburbs we should work to improve them. Besides connecting them better to their cities and the countrysides we should try to end their segregation of rich and poor . . .

Stretton's argument is no less pertinent today than it was 25 years ago. The present consolidation policies serve to deepen the division between rich and poor, to intensify their segregation and mark it with the creation of extensive areas of lower quality built environment.

To some degree the proponents of high density living and the kinds of *urban lifestyle* they yearn for, and which they claim results from it, simply express a variant of cultural cringe. It is as though they argue indirectly that the form of urban development which has evolved in Australia reflecting the climate, level of economic development, way of life and cultural expression is inferior to that overseas.

The *demographic* arguments for consolidation in the claims that the form of Australian cities does not reflect the wants and needs of the households which live in them are not supported by the behaviour of those households. No amount of coercion or promulgation of elitist nostrums will change that.

It is hard to escape the conclusion that the environmental argument for consolidation achieved the saliency it did because governments were determined to make some concessions to the environmental interests in public life. It is clear that Australian cities have some significant environmental problems and that we should address them. But what seems to have happened is that in place of a considered review of the problems and an exploration of what might be done to ameliorate them we have had what amounts to a moral panic. Solutions to pollution problems have been proffered and adopted with scant regard for scientific evidence either about the extent of the problems and their sources or any understanding of the history of the cities and why they take their form. Moreover, there is little scientific evidence that the solutions proposed to cope with environmental stress can or will have the beneficial effects claimed. The more extreme activists have played on fear and they have offered doomsday scenarios to support their nostrums. Governments desperate for the support of the *green vote* have simply adopted environmental arguments without subjecting them to a conventional prudent sceptical review in order to demonstrate their *green* credentials.

Although the consolidation policy was justified in terms of claimed reductions in infrastructure costs, closer fit between the demand for and supply of housing, reductions in environmental stresses and improved choice, its proponents have produced little evidence of the policy's *success* in meeting these objectives but rather have resorted to claims that the ability to market medium density housing is evidence of the success of the policy.

We have argued here that it is possible to reduce demand for infrastructure investment without necessarily reducing urban amenity and that this can be done with a felicitous reduction in environmental stress. This would require a change in the way most infrastructure services are provided and funded. Such an approach would be neutral as to form of housing but would ensure that the servicing and environmental costs associated with each would be met by the households which occupied them.

There is increasing evidence of resistance to the consolidation policy:

- local authorities in New South Wales have increasingly sought to be exempted from the dual occupancy provisions of SEPP 25;
- there is growing opposition to medium density housing in Brisbane and redevelopment and dual occupancy proposals in Melbourne;
- community groups and citizen action groups have increasingly opposed redevelopment and dual occupancy proposals in the Australian Capital Territory;
- developers have taken to assuring potential buyers that their developments contain only *standard sized blocks* and that no medium density housing will be allowed in them.

Communities such as Balmain in Sydney have engaged in major battles with developers and the State government to preserve their territory (Bonyhady 1995). In Canberra community opposition to the policy forced the Australian Capital Territory Government, late in 1994, to significantly modify its policy.

As they are presently framed, housing and urban policies are more likely to reduce the housing options and standards of the lower-middle and lower income members of the community. The policies are based on a flawed analysis and misrepresentation of the facts. The figures on average house size are so unreliable that they can form no basis for a sensible housing policy and in any event the focus on average size of new houses is irrelevant as is most of the *demographic* justification for consolidation. Apart from a small number of demonstration projects, the quality of dwellings and urban space actually produced under the policy is clearly below that resulting from the traditional approach to development.

The arguments about choice of either housing or lifestyle ignore the fact that people already have, and exercise, choice. The *pro choice* arguments are based on the promulgation of elitist romantic notions of urban life which are not based on rigorous analysis of what households have or aspire to.

The consolidation policy has no small ambition. It is designed to make a break with the history of urban Australia by changing the form of urban areas. It is based on the notion that there is some dichotomy between the development of the central city areas and the suburbs which must be dissolved. There is no recognition that the suburbs are integral parts of the metropolis, that they always have been and that we cannot consider Australian metropolitan areas without recognising the interconnectedness of the central city to its suburbs—the one cannot exist without the other, they are not alternatives. The present policy is at once reactionary because it is predicated on archaic notions of a highly centralised city which fail to recognise the changes which have been wrought on the city's structure as it has grown and new technologies have been adopted, and radical because it presupposes that the community *should* and that it *can be made* to change its aspirations and behaviour. The public has not been engaged in any systematic debate on whether the changes proposed are desirable nor have the infrastructure, environmental or demographic arguments made in support of the policy been convincing.

Continued pursuit of the policy will lead to increasing polarisation of the cities. Australian cities already exhibit elements of the *walling off* or *gating* of upper income higher quality areas evident in cities in the United States of America. Consolidation will accelerate the process of spatial separation of social groups and physically define them in ways which have largely been avoided to date.

Australian cities are faced with some significant problems not the least of which are the environmental stresses to which they are subjected. The primary cause of environmental stress is the number of people behaving in a way which undervalues the impact of their actions on the environment. The strategic objective must be to reduce the extent to which people behave in this way. If the primary objective is to reduce environmental stress the question must be: which mechanism is most likely to achieve it most readily? A tactical response would be to develop policy which is based on an assessment of its likely effect on achieving the objective. Changes in behaviour are notoriously slow but can be speeded up by the adoption of new technology. The speed with which Australian households took up the motor car, refrigerators, washing machines, television, telephones, videos and home computers all confirm this point.

Changes in approaches to the design, construction and use of buildings are slow. Changes in the use of buildings can be rapid but their energy consumption patterns may change only slowly. On the other hand changes in technology such as cars can be very fast. Even if all new dwellings were built to reflect the current concern over energy consumption it would take a long time to obtain substantial reductions in stress because the rate of change to the housing stock is very slow (additions to the stock are about 1.5 per cent per annum), moreover, houses have very long lives. Modifications to existing houses along the lines suggested in Chapter 3 could speed up the rate of change and therefore savings of energy and water consumption. Changes to other dwelling types are harder to introduce and result in smaller savings. At current rates of construction it would take about one hundred years to build new stock and replace old stock to achieve a stock of housing which had the efficiency characteristics proponents of consolidation desire. Changes in cars, or at least changes to their sources of power, can have even greater effect much more quickly. New technology can be quickly introduced and lead to a significant reduction in energy consumption. The average age of the vehicle stock is about ten years so the introduction of technology such as in the new Volks Wagen cars (the *Australian* 26 August 1994) or the new Volvos (Boethius 1995) could lead to substantial reductions in energy consumption and therefore greenhouse gas emission within a few years.

Energy reductions due to changes in city form are even harder to achieve and slower to introduce than changes in the housing stock because they are directed at the physical outcomes of a complex set of economic and social processes but not the processes themselves.

While the appropriate strategy is the modification of private and public behaviour of people to properly take into account the environmental stresses they create, the appropriate tactics are to focus on those elements which are most amenable to change. That is we should focus on those elements which have a high rate of depreciation. Physically oriented policies such as the present consolidation policy are least likely to achieve the tactical results desired by the politicians or the strategic objective of more equitable, efficient and environmentally less stressed urban areas.

Australian cities have inherited/developed a form of urban development which reflects its cultural and political values and which, it turns out, offers us the best chance of meeting equity, efficiency and newly recognised environmental targets. The form may well be the accidental or felicitous outcome of historical processes but the policy should now be to intentionally preserve and develop those features. The challenge is to recognise that the inefficiencies and environmental stresses which flow from the structure of the city must be tackled by modifying that structure.

It seems increasingly likely that if we do not heed the evidence of stress in the systems which together comprise the entities known as cities we will experience serious environmental degradation—so serious that it may well lead to the end of cities as we know them.

A Consumer's Guide to Planners Speak defines "Improved Housing Choices" as: "For new areas this means we choose the 'appropriate house' for your family type. For established areas it means '[B]ugger your choice', we don't like it and we're going to change it." That seems to sum up present housing policy.

Throughout this discussion of current housing and urban policies alternative approaches to the setting and specification of policy have been set out. It seems apposite however to draw them together and make more explicit the kind of policies which should be articulated.

Various contributors to the debate about the kinds of policies which should be adopted to cope with environmental stress suggest that *no regrets* policies should be adopted. These include policies which:

> [W]ould not only help moderate emissions of greenhouse gases, but would at the same time also result in net economic benefits (or at least no economic cost) to the economy. In other words, it would make good economic sense to undertake these actions irrespective of the benefits of lower greenhouse gas emissions. (Naughten, Bowen & Beck 1993: 271).

While from an economist's perspective this sentiment is laudable, in the *real world* there are few, if any, such options. Nearly all policies have economic effects outside their narrowly targeted areas and nearly all affect groups differently. Some suffer increased costs while others reap benefits. For example, owners of older vehicles would suffer more than owners of newer vehicles if restrictions on vehicle usage according to efficiency were adopted, although older vehicles tend to travel less than newer: occupants of flats would suffer more than occupants of conventional houses if energy costs were increased to encourage more efficient energy consumption to reduce greenhouse emissions. Moreover, policies to reduce greenhouse emissions might well increase environmental stresses in other sub-systems leading to net economic costs which would mean there might well be serious regrets.

The point is, however, that so-called *no regrets* policies might still be appropriate if transition arrangements were made to ensure that individuals or industries were not penalised to achieve the social or community outcomes deemed to be desirable. That is, it still might be appropriate to require the introduction of higher efficiency vehicles if transition help was made available to those with the older vehicles. Changes in housing policies might be appropriate if those living in the lower efficiency housing were helped during the transition. Current housing and urban policies cannot be described as *no regrets* policies because they incur obvious individual personal costs while leading to no discernible social benefits.

I Shape of Urban Policy

What shape should a national housing and urban development policy take? The answer to this question is not simple and it will only be valid for a particular place and time. It seems however that the policy should be built on four commitments:

The *first commitment* is that all plans and policy proposals should make clear the assumptions, value judgments and trade-offs which they contain. This is a counsel of perfection but it seems reasonable to require the larger, more significant assumptions to be made public so that people can better judge the efficacy of the plans and policies.

The *second commitment* of urban development policy should be to equity. That is, urban development policies and programs should be directed to improving the equity in urban areas in the sense of producing greater equality of outcomes. This can be done by:

- ensuring more equal access to housing
- developing and enforcing regulations setting minimum standards of housing and urban services
- reducing locational inequity in the distribution of jobs
- ensuring more equal access to health and welfare services and facilities
- ensuring more equal access to cultural facilities and services
- ensuring more equal access to recreational facilities including parks and open space
- ensuring more equal access to public administration.

The *third commitment* should be to the development of urban areas in a manner which reduces environmental stress. That is, policy must be directed to abatement of all the sources of environmental stress wherever possible, and not just to global warming (Rosenberg et al 1989). This can be achieved by:

- encouraging the collection, storage and use of rainwater
- encouraging the recycling of domestic waste water
- encouraging the composting and mulching of domestic and garden waste
- encouraging food production in urban areas
- encouraging the separation at source of waste materials to facilitate resource recovery and recycling
- imposing noise pollution standards which protect residential amenity
- imposing air pollution standards to protect the health and amenity of residents
- separating industrial from residential development
- encouraging a more efficient use of energy in the construction and operation of buildings and less reliance on non-renewable energy sources
- encouraging the development of more energy efficient forms of transport and less reliance on non renewable energy sources.

The *fourth commitment* should be to develop a more democratic consultative decision making process. This can be achieved by:

- creating more open public processes for informing citizens of development proposals
- creating open processes for the consideration of development proposals
- preserving third party appeal rights against development proposals
- strengthening the role and independence of local government
- decentralising public administration
- devolving political power of Commonwealth and State governments to regional centres
- accepting the legitimate role of government to intervene in investment in urban areas.

Formulating urban policies to embody these commitments and designing programs to implement them and to provide urban services efficiently necessarily leads to trade offs—it leads to adaptive responses under which we attempt first to pursue abatement and then development policies which accommodate to the pressures and stresses. It would lead to an evolutionary process in which the policies would be continuously developed as both the scientific knowledge of both social processes and natural phenomena developed and community understanding of them progressed.

So what would an alternative urban policy which most closely met the commitments look like?

II Alternative Urban Policy

Government policy would be directed to increase the supply of public housing through a variety of community-based organisations and distributed through the urban areas. The housing could be rented on an averaged cost recovery basis.

All housing developments would be closely coordinated with the creation of employment and the provision of community facilities. Housing would be designed, oriented, equipped and constructed to minimise the requirement for heating by non-renewable fuels. Policy would not be based on reaction to superficial and irrelevant correlations between changes in the demographic structure of the population and the distribution of dwelling sizes in the housing stock.

Government policy would be directed to preserving the traditional form of Australian cities. Redevelopment by demolition of existing buildings would only be permitted where it can be shown that the buildings have reached the end of their structural life and that the redevelopment would result in savings of operational energy which outweighed the embodied energy costs of their refurbishment or replacement or where the buildings were so obsolete it would cost more to restore rather than replace them. Where it is necessary to improve the structural efficiency of an urban area suitable locations for development to higher density would be identified where that was an appropriate form. Blanket provisions for rights to dual occupancy development would be withdrawn. Conservation powers would be strengthened and would include the confiscation of property on which demolition or development occurred without permission.

Public ownership of land through the development or conversion phase should be encouraged, especially for areas designated for redevelopment. A land development fund should be created for this purpose. Surpluses from the conversion and development process should be applied to the provision of community facilities. Where redevelopment of an area was appropriate a public planning process would identify the disposition of uses, explore whether the existing subdivision pattern was apposite and, where changes in use were proposed, take the land into public ownership during the redevelopment phase but reselling the land in its newly designated land use. There could be political difficulties with this proposal but it should be recognised that for any strategy to be workable the question of how to assemble land for development or redevelopment has to be put back on the agenda. It is probably the only way governments can secure their objectives of more equitable and efficient development which also meets acceptable design standards.

A series of sub centres in each metropolitan area would be identified to which commercial and cultural development would be directed. This task would be made easy in most metropolitan areas because sub centres have already developed in them—it needs simply to reinforce them and to select others. Government administration would be decentralised to these centres and could even be accompanied by a substantial degree of devolution of responsibility. Where appropriate, local government would be reorganised so that the centres were the *natural* focus of local government activity and administration. Cultural and recreational facilities provided by government would be developed or focussed at these centres. The transport system, including the public transport system, would be developed to focus on and connect these centres to one another forming a network throughout the urban area. In some cases the public transport connections would be by high volume fixed track transport modes. All private sector proposals for major retailing or office developments would be directed to one of the centres to develop each in balance with its catchment population. Further development of the CBDs would be strongly discouraged. Location and time specific road pricing would be introduced to generate the funds to develop the road system, to ensure its more efficient development and use and to minimise environmental stress.

Regional development policy would encourage the growth of non-metropolitan centres by reducing the apparent economic disadvantages of smaller centres by introducing resource rents and congestion pricing into service provision.

Regional groupings of local government should be given funds by the Commonwealth, allocated according to their relative disadvantage in access to facilities and services, to enable them to overcome their disadvantage. The regional groupings of local governments themselves to decide on the priorities for the development of the services and facilities.

The water supply, drainage and sewerage system would be changed to encourage and make better use of the rain falling on the urban areas. Households would be encouraged to collect and store rainwater and to use it for domestic and garden purposes. Development charges for water supply, drainage and sewerage would be dropped. All new developments would be required to ensure that no more runoff came from and its *peak flow* was no higher after development than before. Recycling of water would be encouraged in dwellings and public parks and gardens would be watered only with recycled water. This would change the present water supply system by incorporating a *cascade* system in which water treatment was carried out locally and the treated water was used for parks, gardens and toilet flushing.

An education program would be mounted to show households how to make better use of water both in their dwellings and on their gardens. A user pays system of water pricing which would include a resource rent would be introduced and properties would be charged for drainage based on their runoff. There are some difficulties associated with measuring and metering runoff which would need to be overcome. Pricing of sewage effluent could raise problems of compliance so illegal discharges to the sewerage and drainage systems would be heavily penalised. Industrial and commercial firms would be further encouraged to use recycled water and they would be charged for water according to use and for sewage effluent according to volume and difficulty of treatment. Sewage sludge would be composted to produce a low grade fertiliser which would be used on public parks and gardens and, where appropriate, in farming.

The method of paying for and collecting household solid wastes would be changed to encourage composting of kitchen and garden wastes and the at-source-separation of recoverable and recyclable materials. An education program would be mounted to show households how wastes may be composted in the best and safest manner. Charges would be levied according to the volume of material collected from households. Industrial and commercial firms would be charged tipping fees for depositing wastes at landfill sites according to its volume, toxicity and complexity. Industry would be encouraged to make use of *waste* materials.

Households would be encouraged to produce some of their own food. This would be achieved by educating households on appropriate gardening practices including how to mulch their gardens to reduce water use and to reduce runoff. Local governments might need to be encouraged to facilitate local seed exchanges, the sharing of garden tools and the sale or barter of surplus food. Households would be encouraged to plant trees and shrubs and to develop gardens to use the mulch produced by composting to reduce watering and runoff. Community-based gardening groups should be encouraged to provide advice on the planting of appropriate trees and shrubs. Local authorities should be encouraged to plant trees in parks and public spaces for the enhancement of amenity, for reduction of environmental stress and for production of wood for fuel.

The encouraging aspect of this policy prescription is that elements of the package are being advocated by different groups and in some cases *bits* of it are being implemented by State and local governments. The sad and worrying aspect is that some of the major elements are resisted by major interest groups such as the water authorities which seem more interested in pursuing privatisation which will limit the ability of cities to pursue better servicing or environmental stress minimisation strategies. Another sad feature of the present situation is that neither governments nor their oppositions seem to take a large or holistic enough view from a long enough perspective to enable them to articulate a comprehensive strategy.

APPENDIX

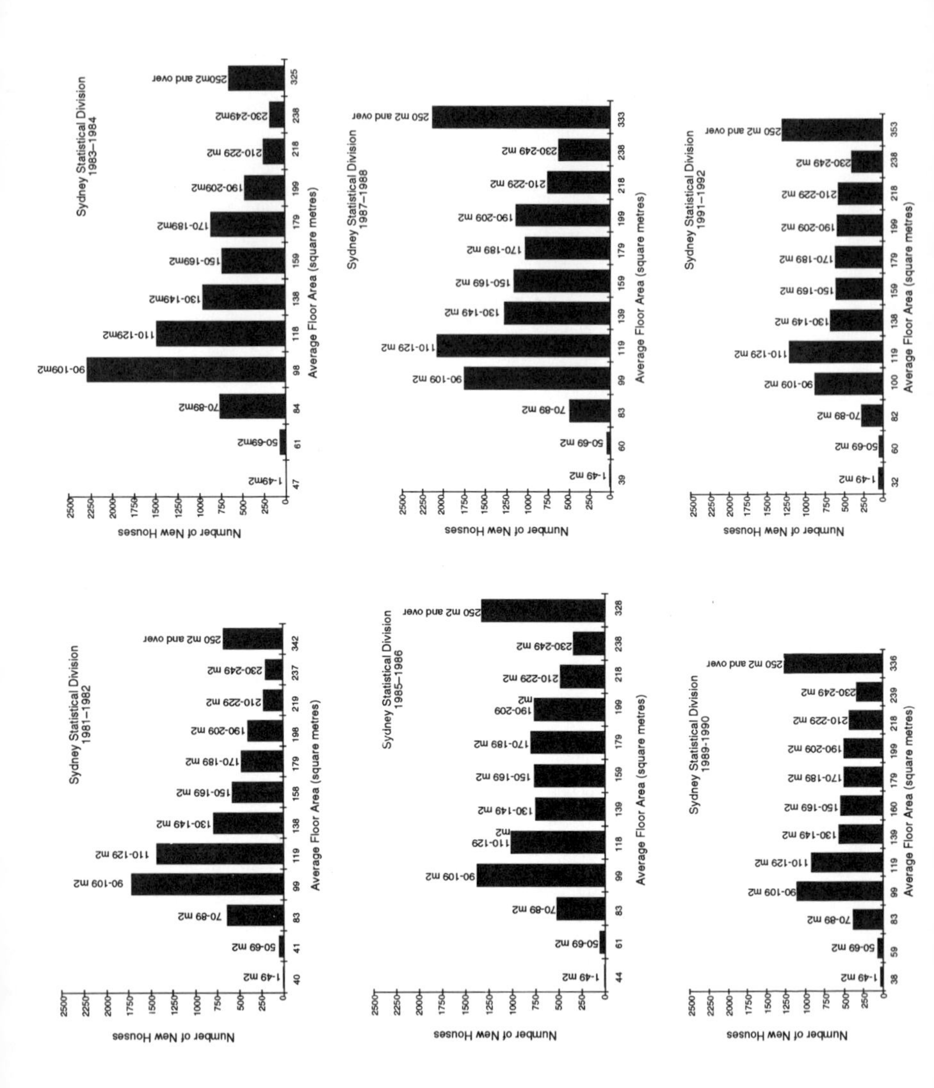

Figure 1 Distribution of Average Size of New Houses: Sydney 1981-1982 to 1991-1992

Source: Australian Bureau of Statistics, Building Approvals, New South Wales, Tables, 3,4 and 6 [unpublished data]; Australia and State Year Books

Note: All data is for finacial year; houses in 'not stated' floor area category are included in count of houses but not included in calculation of average floor area for each year; 1981-1982 – floor area data was missing for one category in the September quarter, all data for this quarter was therfore omitted from calculations for 1981-1982.

APPENDIX

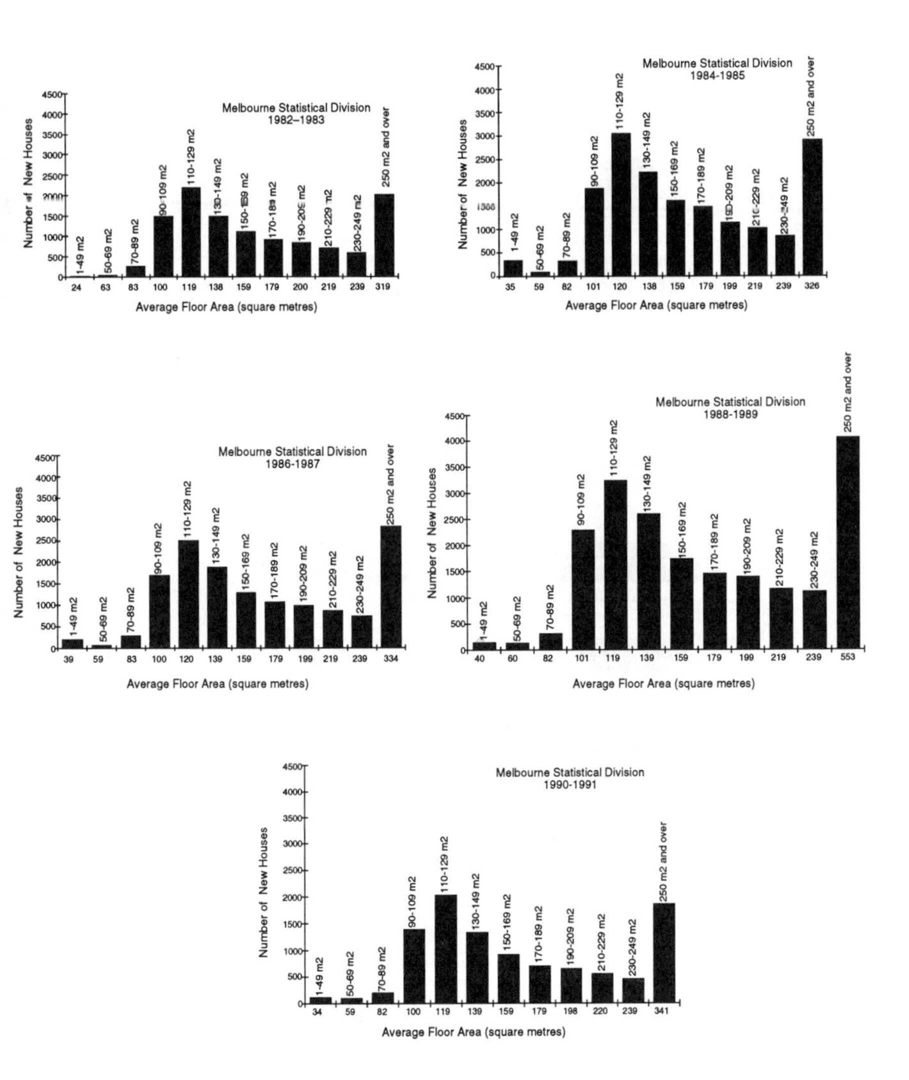

Figure 2 Distribution of Average Size of New Houses: Melbourne 1982-1983 to 1990-1991

Source: Australian Bureau of Statistics, Building Approvals, New South Wales, Tables, 3,4 and 6 [unpublished data]; Australia and State Year Books

Note: All data is for finacial year; houses in 'not stated' floor area category are included in count of houses but not included in calculation of average floor area for each year;.

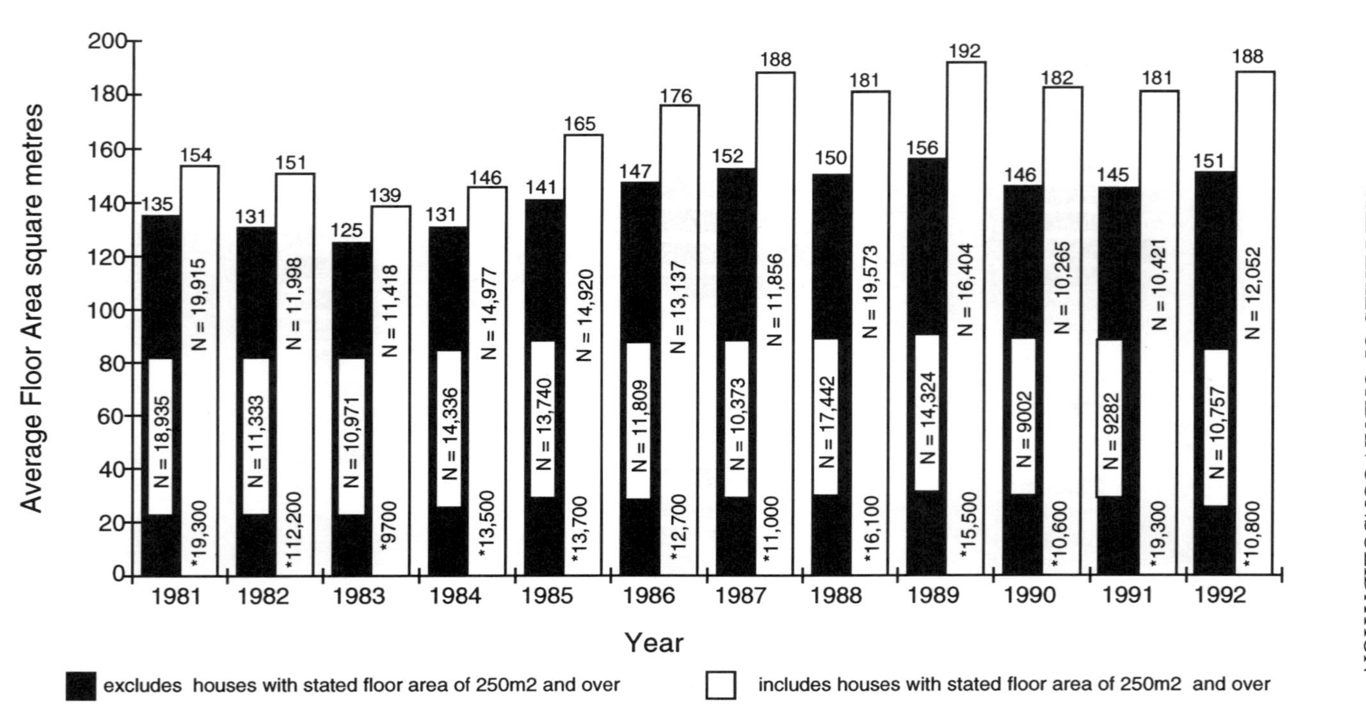

Figure 3 Average Size (average floor area: square metres): New Houses: Sydney 1981 - 1992

Source: Australian Bureau of Statistics , Building Approvals New South Wales, Table 3, 4, and 6 [unpublished data]; Australia and State Year Books

Note: Houses in 'not stated' floor area category are included in count of houses but are not included in calculation of average floor area for each year; 1981 to 1992 – financial year data; 1983 – annual data; floor area data was missing for one category in the 1981-1982 September quarter – all data for this category was therefore omitted from calculations for 1981–1982; asterisked figures are commencements for the same period.

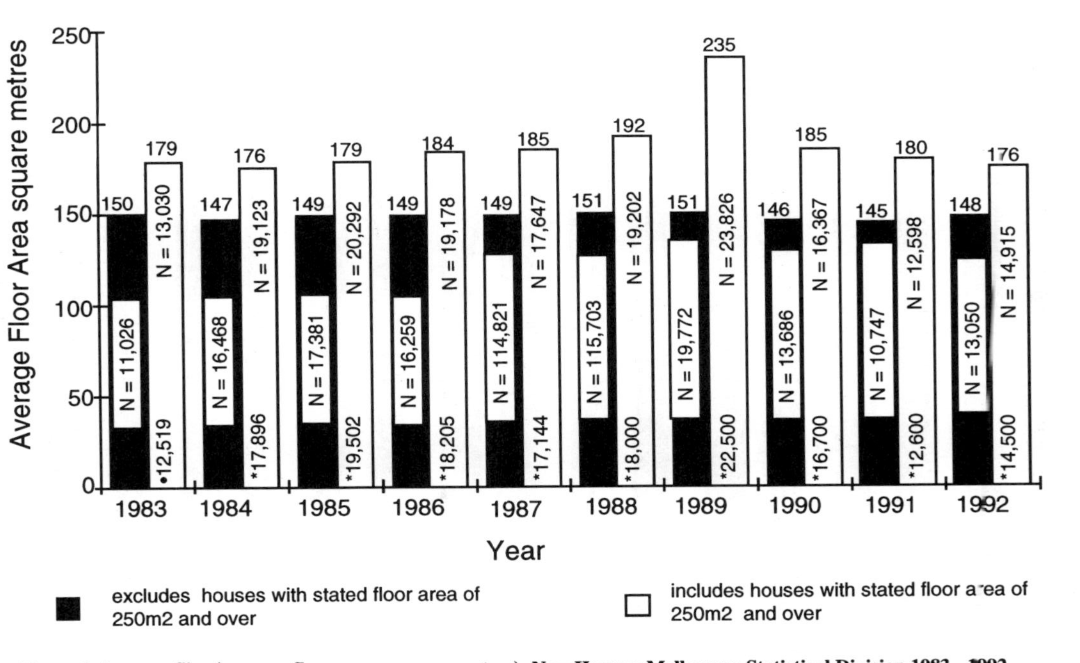

Figure 4 Average Size (average floor area : square metres): New Houses: Melbourne Statistical Division 1983 - 1992
Source: Australian Bureau of Statistics, Building Approvals Tables 3, 4 and 6 [unpublished data]; Australia and State Year Books
Note: Houses in 'not stated' floor area category are included in count of houses but are not included in calculation of average floor area for each year; 1983–annual data; 1984–1992–financial year data; asterisked figures are for commencements for the same period.

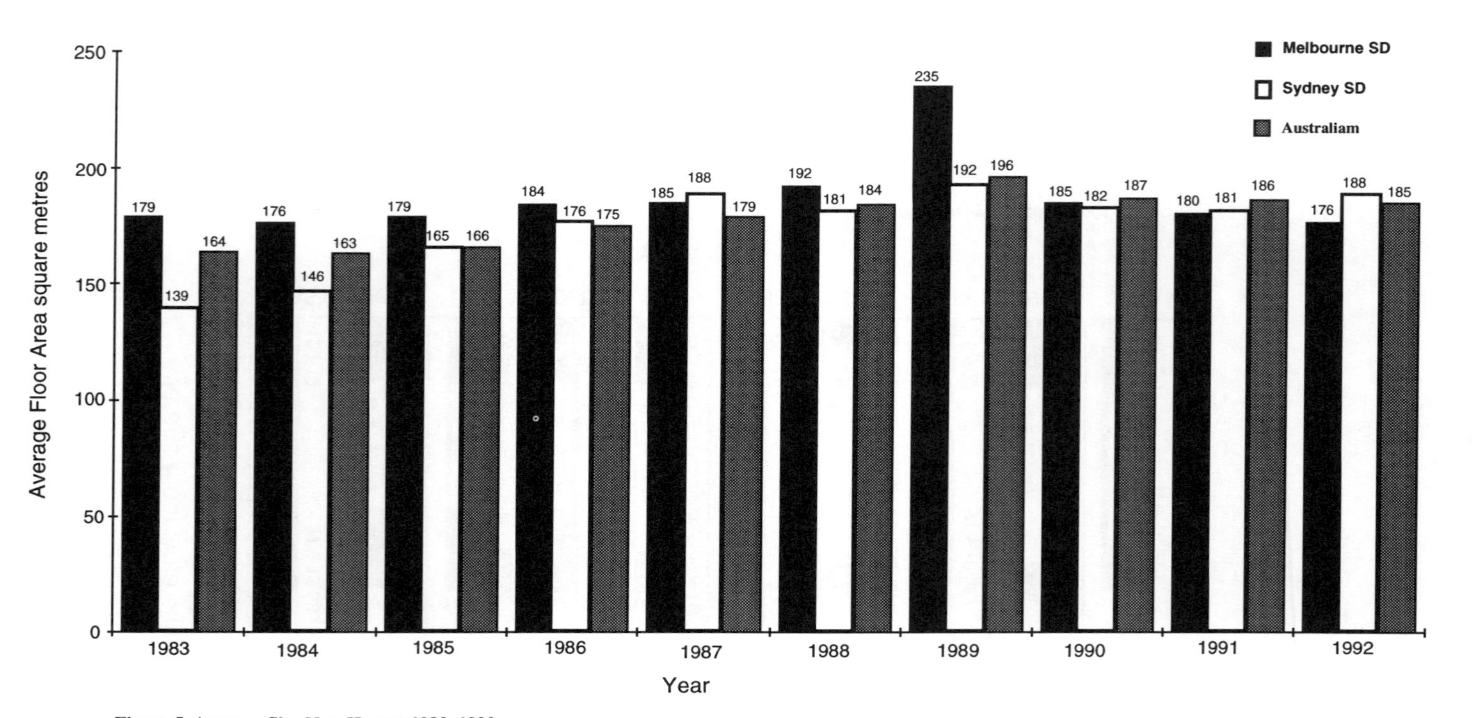

Figure 5 Average Size New Houses 1983–1992
Source: Australian Bureau of Statistics, Building Approvals Tables 3 , 4 and 6 [unpublished data]. Australia and State Year Books
Note: Houses in 'not stated' floor area category are included in count of houses but are not included in calculation of average floor area for each year; 1983 annual data; 1984–1992 financial year data.

BIBLIOGRAPHY

Aina, TK 1990, "The politics of sustainable development", in *The Living City: Towards a Sustainable Future*, (eds) D Cadman & G Payne, Routledge.

Alexander, I 1992, Urban consolidation: good theory bad practice, Paper presented to City of Perth Getting Together Forum, Council House, 18 October.

Altshuler, AA & Gomez-Ibanez, JA 1993, *Regulation for Revenue*, Brookings Institution.

Anderton, N & Lloyd, CJ 1993, *Housing Australia: An Analysis of the 1986 Census*, Australian Housing Research Council.

—— nd, *The Residential Histories and Housing Careers of Australians: An Event History Analysis*, Australian Housing Research Council.

Ashton, P 1993, *The Accidental City: Planning Sydney Since 1788*, Hale & Iremonger.

Australia, Parliament 1955, Development of Canberra, Report from the Senate Select Committee, [Senator JA McCallum, Chairman], Canberra.

Australian Bureau of Agricultural and Resource Economics (ABARE) 1991, *Projections of Energy Demand and Supply: Australia 1990–1991 to 2004–2005*, AGPS.

—— 1993, *Energy: Demand and Supply Projections, Australia 1992–1993 to 2004–2005*, AGPS.

Australian Bureau of Statistics 1981, 1981 Census of Population and Housing, Cross Classified Characteristics of Persons and Dwellings, Cat No 2452.0.

—— 1991, Survey of Motor Vehicle Use, Cat No 9208.0.

—— 1992, *Housing Australia: A Statistical Overview, 1992*, Cat No 1320.0.

—— 1994, *Home Production of Selected Foodstuffs*, Australia 1991–1992, Cat No 7110.0.

—— 1994, *Renters in Australia*, Cat No 4138.0.

—— various years, *Year Book Australia*, Cat No 1301.0.

1986–1987 National Energy Survey: Energy Consumption in Industry, Australia, Cat No 8217.0.

—— *Characteristics of Dwellings Australia* 1990, Standard Tables From the 1990 Survey of Income and Housing Costs and Amenities, Cat No 4133.0.40.001.

—— *Community Participation in Energy Conservation, Victoria, October 1990.* Cat No 4120.2.

—— *Directory of Energy Related Statistics 1992*, Cat No 1107.0.

—— *Directory of Energy Related Statistics 1992*, Cat No 1107.0.

——*Domestic Appliance and Energy Usage, South Australia, October 1990*, Cat No 8207.4.

—— *Domestic Energy and Firewood Usage, Tasmania 1987*, Cat No 8204.6.

—— *Domestic Energy Use, New South Wales, October 1989*, Cat No 8217.1.

—— *Domestic Firewood and Coal Usage, Tasmania 1985*, Cat No 8204.6.

—— *Domestic Heating and Firewood Usage, South Australia, October 1989*, Cat No 8210.4

—— *National Energy Survey: Annual Consumption of Reticulated Energy by Households, Australia 1985–1986*, Cat No 8213.0.

—— *National Energy Survey: Household Appliances, Facilities and Insulation, Australia, November 1980*, Cat No 8212.0.

—— National Energy Survey, Household Energy Consumption, Australia 1982–1983, Cat No 8213.0.

—— *National Energy Survey, Weekly Reticulated Energy and Appliance Usage Patterns by Season, Households, Australia 1985–1986*, Cat No 8218.0.

—— *New South Wales Energy Survey, October 1984: Part 2, Household Energy Consumption,* Cat No 8212.1.
—— *New South Wales Energy Survey: Part 1, Household Appliances, Facilities, Insulation and Appliance Acquisition, October 1984,* Cat No 8211.1.
—— *New South Wales Year Book,* Cat No 1300.1.
—— *Queensland Year Book* , Cat No 1301.3.
—— *South Australian Year Book* , Cat No 1301.4.
—— *Survey of Household Energy Sources, Tasmania: August 1975,* Cat No
—— *Survey of Household Energy Sources, Tasmania: June 1978,* Cat No 8204.6.
—— *Tasmanian Year Book,* Cat No 1301.6.
—— *Victorian Year Book,* Cat No 1301.2.
—— *Western Australian Year Book* , Cat No 1301.5.
Australian Conservation Foundation, *Habitat,* 20, 4, November 1992.
Australian Housing Industry Development Council (AHIDC) 1991, The Structure of the Housing Industry, Report prepared by ACIL Australia Pty Ltd for the Commonwealth Department of Health, Housing & Community Services, AGPS.
—— 1994a, Cost Differentials in the Housing Industry, Part 1 Labour Market Issues, Occasional Series No 6, Report prepared by Industry Development Consultancy Services, AGPS.
—— 1994b, Cost Differentials in the Housing Industry, Part 2, Regulations and Charges, Occasional Series No 7, Report prepared by WD Woodhead, Division of Building, Construction and Engineering & G Zillante, School of Bulding and Planning University of South Australia, AGPS.
Australian Institute of Health and Welfare 1995, *Australia's Welfare: Services and Assistance,* AGPS.
Australian Labor Party 1982, Australian Labor Party, Platform Constitution and Rules.
Australian Model Code for Residential Development: Guidelines for Urban Housing (AMCORD URBAN) 1992, Department of Health, Housing and Community Services, AGPS.
Australian Urban and Regional Development Review (AURDR) 1993a, "Metropolitan planning in Australia", Workshop paper No 3, Proceedings of a workshop held by the Hon Brian Howe, MP Deputy Prime Minister, Minister for Housing, Local Government and Community Services, and prepared by National Capital Planning Authority, Department of Housing and Regional Development, Canberra, March.
—— 1993b, "New homes for old", Workshop paper No 1, Proceedings of a workshop held by the Hon Brian Howe, MP Deputy Prime Minister, Minister for Housing, Local Government and Community Services, and prepared by Sandy Haley, Department of Housing and Regional Development, Canberra, December.
—— 1993c, "Transport and urban development", Workshop paper No 2, Proceedings of a workshop held by the Hon Brian Howe, MP Deputy Prime Minister, Minister for Housing, Local Government and Community Services and prepared by the National Capital Planning Authority), Department of Housing and Regional Development, Canberra, December.
—— 1994, *Australian Cites and Regions: A National Approach,* Information paper 1, Department of Housing and Regional Development, Canberra.

—— 1995a, *Places for Everyone: Social Equity in Australian Cities and Regions*, Research report 1, AURDR.
—— 1995b, *Smart Planning Not Sprawl*, Discussion paper 5, AURDR.
Babbage, D 1993, "The impact of medium density housing on adjacent property values", *Urban Futures Journal*, 3(2): 30-32.
Bannister, D, Watson, S & Wood, C 1994, The relationship between energy use and urban form, Working paper 10, Planning and Development Research Centre, University College.
Barbier, EB 1987, "The concept of sustainable economic development", *Environmental Conservation* 14 (2) Summer.
Bell, DA 1991, "Office location—city or suburbs?: travel impacts arising from office relocation from city to suburbs", *Transportation*, 18: 239.
Better Cities 1991, *Building Better Cities Program, Victorian Agreement.*
Better Cities (Australia) 1992, *National Developments 1991–1992*, Housing and Regional Development Program, Commonwealth Department of Health, Housing & Community Services, Canberra.
—— 1994, *Better Cities: Mid Program Report*, Department of Housing and Regional Development, Canberra.
—— 1995, *Better Cities: National Status Report*, Department of Housing and Regional Development, Canberra.
Better Cities (Australian Capital Territory) nd, Territory brochures
Better Cities (New South Wales) nd, State brochures.
Better Cities (Queensland) nd, State brochures.
Better Cities (South Australia) nd, State brochures.
Better Cities (Victoria) 1992, *Developments 1991–1992*, Housing and Regional Development Program, Commonwealth Department of Health, Housing & Community Services, Canberra.
—— nd, State brochures.
Better Cities (Western Australia) nd, State brochures
Birrell, R 1991, Infrastructure Costs on the Urban Fringe, Background papers on urban and regional issues, Economic Planning Advisory Council.
Black, J 1982a, "Energy and social change: the transport sector in Australia", in*Liquid Fuels in Australia: A Social Science Research Perspective*, (ed) J Black, Pergamon Press.
—— (ed) 1982b, *Liquid Fuels in Australia: A Social Sience Research Perspective*, Pergamon Press.
Boethius, O 1995, "The Volvo environmental concept car", *Australian Planner*, 32(4): 222.
Bonyhady, T 1995, "The battle for Balmain", in *Australian Cities: Issues, Strategies and Policies for Urban Australia in the 1990s*, (ed) P Troy, Cambridge University Press.
Boothroyd, P 1988, "On using environmental assessment to promote fair sustainable development", *The Role of Environmental Assessment in Promoting Sustainable Development: Three Views*, UBC Planning Papers, Discussion paper 13, University of British Columbia, Vancouver, June.
Bourassa, S 1993, A model of housing tenure choice in Australia, Urban Research Program, Working paper 39, Research School of Social Sciences, Australian National University, August.

Bourassa, S, Greig, A & Troy, P 1995, "The limits of housing policy: home ownership in Australia", *Housing Studies*, 10(1): 83.

Breheny, M (ed) 1992, *Sustainable Development and Urban Form*, Pion.

Brindle, R 1992, "Transport and land use: a 'neo-modern' approach", *Proceedings 16th ARRB Conference, Part 6: 111*, Australian Road Research Board, Vermont South, Victoria.

Brotchie, J, Batty, M, Blakely, E, Hall, P & Newton, P (eds) 1995, *Cities in Competition: Productive and Sustainable Cities for the 21st Century*, Longman Australia Pty Ltd.

Brotchie, J, Gipps, PG & Newton, P 1995, "Urban land use, transport and the information economy: metropolitan employment, journey to work trends and their implications for transport", *Urban Futures*, 17: 37.

Brown, N 1995, 'A cliff of white cleanliness': decorating the home, defining the self, Urban Research Program, Working paper 48, Research School of Social Sciences, Australian National University, April.

Brown-May, A 1995, The highway of civilisation and commonsense: street regulation and the transformation of social space in 19th century Melbourne, Urban Research Program, Working paper 49, Research School of Social Sciences, Australian National University, April.

Brundtland, GH 1987, *Our Common Future*, Report of the World Commission on Environment and Development [Brundtland report].

Bureau of Transport and Communications Economics (BTCE) 1991a, *Compendium of Australian Research into Transport and the Urban Environment*, Information paper 37, AGPS.

—— 1991b, Greenhouse gas emissions in Australian transport, Working paper 1, Submission to the Industry Commission Inquiry into the Costs and Benefits of Reducing Greenhouse Gas Emissions, Canberra, May.

—— 1995a, *Greenhouse Gas Emissions in Australian Transport in 1900 and 2000*, Occasional paper 110, [Prepared by Dr Leo Dobes], AGPS.

—— 1995b, *Greenhouse Gas Emissions from Australian Transport; Long Term Projections*, Report 88, AGPS.

Burnley, IH 1983, "Trends in Sydney's population", *Australian Planner*, April–May, 41.

Cadman, D & Payne, G 1990, *The Living City: Towards a Sustainable Future*, Routledge.

Caldwell, LK 1984, "Political aspects of ecologically sustainable development", *Environmental Conservation*, 11(4): 299.

Castles, F 1985, *The Working Class and Welfare*, Allen & Unwin.

Census of the Commonwealth of Australia 1911, 3rd April, Vol III Detailed Tables.

—— 1921, 4th April, Vol II Detailed Tables and Statistician's Report.

—— 1933, 30 June, Vol III Detailed Tables Parts XXIX–XXXVII.

—— 1947, 30 June, Vol III Detailed Tables Parts XX–XXVII, Statistician's Report Australian Life Table.

—— 1961, 30 June, Census Bulletin 22, Summary of Dwellings for Australia.

—— 1971, Bulletin 2, Part 9 Summary of Dwellings for Australia.

Commonwealth Environment Protection Agency, Australia 1994a, *An Analysis of Environmental Impact Assessment Practices and Procedures in Australian States and Territories*, Review of Commonwealth Environment Impact Assessment, May.

—— 1994b, *Analysis of Environmental Impact Assessment Practices and Procedures in Other Countries*, Review of Commonwealth Environment Impact Assessment, May.

—— 1994c, *Assessment of Cumulative Impact and Strategic Assessment in Environmental Impact Assessment*, Review of Commonwealth Environment Impact Assessment, [prepared by JD Court and Associates Pty Ltd and Guthrie Consulting], (authors John D Court, Colin, J Wright and Alasdair C, Guthrie) May.

—— 1994d, *Executive Summaries of Consultants' Reports*, Review of Commonwealth Environment Impact Assessment, May.

—— 1994e, *Public Inquiry Process*, Review of Commonwealth Environment Impact Assessment, May.

—— 1994f, *Public Participation in the Environmental Impact Assessment Process: Input into the Public Review of the Commonwealth Environmental Impact Assessment Process*, Review of Commonwealth Environment Impact Assessment, [prepared by Kinhill Engineers Pty Ltd] May.

—— 1994g, *Social Impact Assessment*, Review of Commonwealth Environment Impact Assessment, May.

Council on Environmental Quality 1975, "The cost of sprawl", *Ekistics*, 40: 239.

Daly, H & Cobb, J 1989, *For the Common Good: Redirecting the Economy Toward Community, The Environment, and a Sustainable Future*, Beacon Press.

Davison, B, Kendig, H, Stephens, F, Merrill, V 1993, *It's My Place*, A Report on the Study, Options and Preferences: Older People and their Homes, AGPS.

Dear, M, 1989, "Privatization and the rhetoric of planning practice", *Environment and Planning* , D7: 449.

Deni Greene Consulting Services 1991, *Overcoming Barriers to Energy Efficiency*, A Series of Greenhouse Studies No 7, Prepared for Dept of the Arts, Sport, the Environment, Tourism & Territories, Canberra.

Department of Environment & Planning (NSW) 1988, *Sydney Into Its Third Century: Metropolitan Strategy for the Sydney Region*, Dept of Environment & Planning, Sydney.

Department of Health, Housing & Community Services, 1992–1995, *Development Now*, quarterly publication, various issues.

Department of Health, Housing & Community Services 1992a, *Annual Report 1991–1992*.

—— 1992b, Submission to the Industry Commission Inquiry: Taxation and Financial Policy Impacts on Urban Settlement, June.

—— 1993, *Structure of the Housing Industry*, Report prepared by ACIL Australia for the Housing Industry Development Strategy, Occasional series No 5, AGPS.

Department of Health, Housing & Community Services, Australian Housing Industry Development Council 1992, *Structure of the Residential Land Development Industry*, Report prepared by ACIL Australia Pty Ltd, AGPS.

Department of Industry Technology and Commerce (DITAC) 1988, *Review of Residential Development Approval Processes*, Discussion paper, July.

—— 1990, *Australian Model Code for Residential Development*, Edition 2, AGPS.

—— 1992, *Managing Stormwater: The Untapped Resource*, Research report 3, Environmental Technology Committee, DITAC.

Department of Industry, Technology and Commerce & Department of Health, Housing & Community Services 1991a, *Housing Costs Study 1, 2, 3* (see Travers Morgan Pty Ltd & Applied Economics Pty Ltd.

—— 1991b, *Housing Costs Study Overview* (see Housing Costs Steering Committee).

Department of Industry, Technology & Regional Development (DITRD) 1993a, *Developing Australia: A Regional Perspective*, A Report to the Government by the Taskforce on Regional Development, vol 1, Canberra.
—— 1993b, *Developing Australia: A Regional Perspective*, A report to the Government by the Taskforce on Regional Development, vol 2, Canberra.
Department of Planning New South Wales, 1987–1994, *State Regional Environment Plans.*
—— 1994, *Cities for the 21st Century: Integrated Urban Management for Sydney, Newcastle, the Central Coast and Wollongong*, NSW Dept of Planning.
Department of Planning & Development, Victoria 1993, *The Low Energy Suburb, Greenhouse Neighbourhood Project*, Summary Report prepared for the Victorian Government's Department of Planning and Development Environment Protection Authority Energy Victoria, by Loder and Bayly Consulting Group, RJ Naim & Partners Pty Ltd, Sustainable Solutions Pty Ltd, PPK Consultants Pty Ltd.
Department of Planning & Housing, Victoria 1992a, *Infrastructure for Urban Development*, Discussion paper, Victorian Housing and Residential Development Plan, Project No 8.
—— 1992b, *Urban Consolidation Initiatives*, Discussion paper, Victorian Housing and Residential Development Plan, Project No 6.
—— 1992c, *Victorian Code for Residential Development—Multi-dwellings*, State Government of Victoria, Melbourne.
—— 1992d, *Victorian Code for Residential Development—Subdivision and Single Dwellings*, State Government of Victoria, Melbourne.
Department of Primary Industries & Energy (Energy Research and Development Corporation) 1990, *Technical Reports and Other Publications: Energy Research*, AGPS.
—— 1991a, *Australian Energy Management News*, Issue No 13, May, AGPS.
—— 1991b, *Issues in Energy Policy: An Agenda for the 1990s*, AGPS.
—— 1995, *Australian Energy Management News*, Issue No 27, May, AGPS.
Department of Resources & Energy 1984, *Energy Demand and Supply: Australia 1960–1961 to 1982–1983*, AGPS.
Department of the Environment, Sport & Territories (DEST) 1994a, *Australian Methods for the Estimation of Greenhouse Gas Emmission and Study on Natural Greenhouse Gas Inventory 1988 & 1990.*
—— 1994b, Summary National Greenhouse Inventory.
Department of Transport, NSW 1993, *Integrated Transport Strategy for Greater Sydney*, First Release for Public Discussion, October.
—— 1995, *Integrated Transport Strategy for the Greater Metropolitan Region*, January.
Development Now (see Department of Health, Housing & Community Services).
Dingle, A & Rasmussen, C 1991, *Vital Connections: Melbourne and its Board of Works 1891–1991*, McPhee Gribble.
Dobes, L 1991, (see Bureau of Transport and Communication Economics 1991).
Dovers, S & Handmer, J 1993, Ignorance and the precautionary priniciple: towards an analytical framework, Paper presented at the Precautionary Principle Conference, Institute of Environmental Studies, University of New South Wales, 20-21 September.
Dovers, S 1994, "A framework for scaling and framing policy problems in sustaiability", *Ecological Economics*, 12: 93.

BIBLIOGRAPHY

Driscoll, S 1994, The reality of dual occupancy, *Urban Scrawl*, 1(5): 3.

Dwyer Leslie Pty Ltd & Hughes Truman Ludlow 1991, *Public Sector Cost Savings of Urban Consolidation*, Final Report, NSW Department of Planning, Sydney Water Board, Dept of Industry, Technology & Commerce.

Ecologically Sustainable Development Steering Committee, Australia 1992, *National Strategy for Ecologically Sustainable Development*, AGPS.

Ecologically Sustainable Development Working Groups 1991a, *Final Report—Agriculture*, AGPS.

—— 1991b, *Final Report—Energy Production*, AGPS.

—— 1991c, *Final Report—Energy Use*, AGPS.

—— 1991d, *Final Report—Fisheries*, AGPS.

—— 1991e, *Final Report—Forest Use*, AGPS.

—— 1991f, *Final Report—Manufacturing*, AGPS.

—— 1991g, *Final Report—Mining*, AGPS.

—— 1991h, *Final Report—Tourism*, AGPS.

—— 1991i, *Final Report—Transport*, AGPS.

Edgar, G 1993, *Dual Occupancy in the Sydney Region*, Planning Research Centre, University of Sydney.

Edwards, M & Madden, R 1991, *Housing Characteristics and Decisions: A Comparative Study of Sydney, Melbourne, Adelaide and Canberra*, National Housing Strategy & Australian Bureau of Statistics, ABS Cat No 8710.0 Canberra.

Ekins, P 1989, "Beyond growth: the real priorities of sustainable development", *Environmental Conservation*, 16(1) Spring.

Elder, G 1975, "Age differentiation and the life course", *Annual Review of Sociology*, 1: 165.

Elder, G 1985, "Perspectives on the life course", in *Life Course Dynamics: Trajectories and Transitions*, (ed) G Elder Jr, Cornell University Press.

Environment Protection Authority (Atmosphere & Energy Policy Unit), Victoria 1994, *Victorian Transport Externalities Study*, A Study Conducted by the EPA in Association with the Bureau of Transport & Communication Economics, and the Commonwealth Department of the Environment, Sport & Territories, Melbourne.

Environmental Management in Developing Countries 1991, Organisation for Economic Co-operation and Development, Paris.

Environmental Planning and Assessment Act 1979 (NSW), (EPAA).

Environmental Policies for the Cities in the 1990s, 1990, Organisation for Economic Co-operation and Development, Paris.

Evans, A 1988, *No Room!, No Room!: The Costs of the British Town and Country Planning System*, London, Occasional Paper No 79, Institute of Economic Affairs, Great Britain.

Fishman, R 1993, "The new American city", *Policy*, Spring: 23.

Fitzgerald, S 1992, *Sydney 1842–1992*, Sydney, Hale & Iremonger.

Frost, L & Dingle, T 1995, "Sustaining suburbia: an historical perspective on Australia's growth", *Australian Cities*, Cambridge University Press.

Gooding, A 1990, *Consolidating for People: The Impact of Urban Consolidation on the Planning and Provision of Human Services*, Western Sydney Regional Organisation of Councils.

Grahn, P (nd), Green structures—the importance for health of nature areas and parks, Planning and Development in Urban Areas Related to Various Patterns of Life – Questions of Infrastruture, University of Agricultural Science Sweden [mimeo].

Green Street Joint Venture 1991, *Attitudes to Housing in Australia*, Market Research Study, DITAC, Canberra.

Greig, A 1995a, Home magazines and modernist dreams: designing the 50s house, Urban Research Program, Working paper 47, Research School of Social Sciences, Australian National University, April.

Greig, A 1995b, *The Stuff Dreams are Made Of*, Melbourne University Press.

Gurney, C 1991, "Ontological security and its place in the home", *People and Physical Environment Research*, 36 April, Special Edition.

Halkett, I 1975, An analysis of the use and design of residential gardens in Adelaide, South Australia, PhD Thesis, Australian National University.

Halkett, I 1976, *The Quarter-Acre block: The Use of Suburban Gardens*, Australian Institute of Urban Studies, Canberra.

Harloe, M 1995, *The People's Home?: Social Rented Housing in Europe and America*, Blackwell.

Harris, SF 1982, "Social aspects of energy in Australia: A social science literature and research review", in *Liquid Fuels in Australia: A Social Science Research Perspective*, (ed) J Black, Pergamon Press.

Harrison, P 1970, "Measuring urban sprawl", in *Analysis of Urban Development, (Tewkesbury Symposium 1970)*, (ed) NF Clark, Special Report No 5, Transport Section, Department of Civil Engineering, University of Melbourne 3.3 – 3.6.

Hayward, D 1986, "The great Australian dream reconsidered: a review of Kemeny", *Housing Studies*, 1(4): 210.

Hendershott, P & Bourassa, S 1992, *Overinvestment in Australian Housing*, National Housing Strategy, Background paper No 9, AGPS.

Hensher, DA 1993, "Socially and environmentally appropriate urban futures for the motor car", *Transportation*, 20: 1.

Hensher, DA 1994, Opportunities to reduce greenhouse gas emissions in the urban passenger transport sector, Institute of Transport Studies Working paper 94-3, Graduate School of Business, University of Sydney.

Hensher, DA & Smith, NB 1986, A structural model of the use of automobiles by households: a case study of urban Australia, *Transport Review*, 6(1): 87.

Holland, G & Holland, I 1991, "Appropriate design decision making, in technology and design", *Proceedings of the 1991 Australian and New Zealand Architectural Science Association*, Adelaide: 197.

Holland, G & Holland, I 1995, "Difficult decisions about ordinary things: being ecologically responsible about timber framing", *Australian Journal of Environmental Management*, 2(3): 157.

Hopkins, A 1994, "The importance of community", *The Australia Institute*, 1, July, Canberra.

Horridge, M 1991, *A General Equilibrium Model of Australia's Second Largest City*, Centre of Policy Studies Discussion paper, Monash University, September.

Horridge 1992, "Land use and commuter transport within Melbourne", *Urban Futures*, Special Issue 5.

Housing Costs Study Steering Committee 1992, *Housing Costs Study: Overview of Study*.

BIBLIOGRAPHY

Howe, Hon B, 1990, *Towards National Approaches to a National Issue*, Paper presented to the Third International Infrastructure Conference, "Infrastructure Investnment in the 1990s", Hilton Hotel, Sydney.

Huges Truman Ludlow & Dwyer Leslie Pty Ltd 1991, *Public Sector Cost Savings of Urban Consolidation*, Appendices to Final Report for New South Wales Department of Planning, Sydney Water Board and Department of Industry Technology and Commerce, February.

Industry Commission (Australia) 1992, *Taxation and Financial Policy Impacts on Urban Settlement*, vols 1 & 2 , AGPS.

—— 1993, Public Housing, Report No 34, November, AGPS.

—— 1994, Urban Transport, Report No 37, February, AGPS.

Institution of Engineers, Australia 1992, *Environmental Principles for Engineers,: Principles for the Engineering Profession for the Planning, Implementation and Management of Engineering Works that are Socially, Ecologically and Economically Sustainable*, Prepared by the National Committee on Environmental Engineering, Barton, ACT.

Jackson, RV & Bridge, H 1987, "Housing", in *Australians: Historical Statistics*, (ed) W Vamplew, Fairfax, Syme & Weldon Associates.

Jacobs, J 1961, *The Death and Life of Great American Cities*, Vintage Books.

James, D 1991 *Economics, Environment and Sustainable Development*, Resource Assessment Commission, Occasional Publication No 1, June, AGPS.

Kemeny, J 1983, *The Great Australian Nightmare: A Critique of Home-Ownership Ideology*, Georgian House.

Kendig, H 1984a, "Housing careers, life cycle and residential mobility: implications for the housing market", *Urban Studies*, 21: 271.

—— 1984b, "The cumulation of inequity: housing costs and income support in old age", *Australian Journal on Ageing*, 3(1): 8.

—— 1990a, "A life course perspective on housing attainment", in *Housing Demography: Linking Demographic Structure and Housing Markets*, (ed) D Meyers, University of Wisconsin.

—— 1990b, Comparative perspectives on housing, ageing and social structure, in *Handbook on Ageing and the Social Sciences*, (eds) R Binstock & L George, Academic Press.

Kendig, H, Paris, B & Anderton, N 1987, *Towards Fair Shares in Australian Housing*, National Non-government Committee for the International Year of Shelter for the Homeless, Canberra.

Kirwan, R 1991a, *Financing Urban Infrastructure: Equity and Efficiency Considerations*, National Housing Strategy Background paper No 4, AGPS.

—— 1991b, "Metropolitan expansion and housing affordability: influences on the cost of housing in Melbourne: a policy analysis: an extract", *Urban Futures* , 1(3): 7.

Kirwan, R & Martin, D with assistance from I Bgugel & M Ball 1972, The economics of urban residential land renewal and improvement, Working paper 77, Centre for Environmental Studies, London.

Kirwan, R (Urban Policy Associates Pty Ltd) 1992, *Financing Urban Infrastructure: Equity and Efficiency Considerations*, Social Justice Research Program into Locational Disadvantage, Prime Minister and Cabinet Report No 1, AGPS.

Knight, RV 1993, "Sustainable development—sustainable cities", *International Social Science Journal*, 135: 35.

Ladd, H 1993, "Population growth, urban density and costs of providing public services", *Urban Studies*, 29(2): 273.
Lamb, R & Holland, G 1994, "Are physical and cultural issues of ecologically sustainable development always compatible?: the Australian housing example of urban consolidation", *People and Physical Environment Research*, 47: 34.
Lansdown, RB 1994, *Australian Capital Territory Residential Development Review*, Report to the Minister for Environment Land and Planning, Canberra.
Lloyd, CJ & Troy, PN 1981, *Innovation and Reaction: The Life and Death of the Department of Urban and Regional Development*, George Allen & Unwin.
Lloyd, CJ, Troy, P & Schreiner, S 1992, *For the Public Health: The Hunter District Water Board 1892–1992*, Longman Cheshire.
Logan, MI 1982, "Energy and social change: The urban sector in Australia", in *Liquid Fuels in Australia: A Social Science Research Perspective*, (ed) J Black, Pergamon Press.
Maher, C 1991, The social justice implications of intra-urban mobility, Seminar paper delivered to Urban Research Program, Research School of Social Sciences, ANU Canberra.
—— 1993, "Household mobility and locational disadvantage: key findings of research into the implications of residential mobility within Australian cities", *Urban Futures Journal*, 3(2): 10.
—— 1994, "Residential mobility, locational disadvantage and spatial inequality in Australian cities", *Urban Policy and Review*, 12(3): 185.
Maher, C, Whitelaw, J, McAllister, A, Francis, R, Palmer, J, Chee, E, & Taylor, P 1992, *Mobility and Locational Disadvantage within Australian Cities: Social Justice Implications of Household Relocation*, AGPS.
Mant, J 1994, (*see* Prime Minister's Urban Design Taskforce 1994).
—— 1995, "Form follows organisation: some suggestions for improving the quality of organisations and urban design", *Urban Futures*, 17, February: 9.
McLoughlin, B 1991, "Urban consolidation and urban sprawl: a question of density", *Urban Policy and Research*, 9(3): 148.
—— 1992, *Shaping Melbourne's Future: Town Planning, the State and Civil Society*, Cambridge University Press.
—— 1993, "Urban consolidation: a modern myth", *Policy*, Spring: 19.
Ministry of Housing & Construction, Victoria and Commonwealth Department of Community Services & Health 1990, *Urban Consolidation: A National Perspective*, Background Discussion Paper for the Special Conference of Housing and Planning Ministers.
Ministry of Transport, Victoria 1981a, *Melbourne Home Interview Travel Survey 1978–1979*, Report 2: Description, prepared by B Cramphorn, Ministry of Transport, Melbourne.
—— 1981b, *Melbourne Home Interview Travel Survey 1978–1979*, Report 3: Comparison, Ministry of Transport, Melbourne.
Morgan, Travers, Pty Ltd & Applied Economics Pty Ltd 1991a, *Housing Costs Study no 1: Costs of New Housing Development*, Australian Building Research Grants Scheme, August.
—— 1991b, *Housing Costs Study no 2: Evaluation of Fringe Development and Urban Consolidation*, Australian Building Research Grants Scheme, August.

—— 1991c, *Housing Costs Study no 3: Determinants of the Prices of Established Housing*, Australian Building Research Grants Scheme, August.

Mullins, P 1981a, "Theoretical perspectives on Australian urbanisation: 1. material components in the reproduction of Australian labour power", *Australian and New Zealand Journal of Sociology*, 17(1): 65.

—— 1981b, "Theoretical perspectives on Australian urbanisation: 2. social components in the reproduction of Australian labour power", *Australian and New Zealand Journal of Sociology*, 17(3): 35.

—— 1987, "Community and urban movements", Sociological Review, 35(2): 347.

Munro-Clark, M 1992, "Attitudinal barriers to an increased level of medium-density development: a review of available evidence", *People and Physical Environment Research*, 41-42: 53.

National Housing Strategy 1991a, *Australian Housing: The Demographic, Economic and Social Environment*, Issues paper 1, AGPS.

—— 1991b, *The Efficient Supply of Affordable Land and Housing: The Urban Challenge*, Issues paper 4, AGPS.

—— 1992a, *Agenda for Action*, AGPS.

—— 1992b, *Housing Choice: Reducing the Barriers*, Issues paper 6, AGPS.

National Shelter 1993, *'Gory Dublin' Costs and Benefits of Public Housing in Australia*, National Shelter, Australia.

—— 1994a, *National Housing Action*, 10 (2) August Special Edition.

—— 1994b, *Public Housing in Australia: Issues and Direction for Change*, National Shelter, Canberra.

Naughten, BR 1993, "Climate change, Australian impacts and economic analysis: comment on Drosdowsky and Maunder", *Climactic Change*, 25: 255.

—— 1994, The role of buses in reducing greenhouse emissions in an energy system wide framework, Australian Institute of Energy International Conference 1994, "Energy, Economics, Environment", Sydney 14-16 March ABARE Conference paper 94(8): 1.

Naughten, BR, Bowen, B & Beck, T 1993, "Energy market failure in road transport: is there scope for 'no regerets' greenhouse gas reduction?", *Climatic Change*, 25: 271.

Naughten, BR, Thorpe, S & Tobler, P 1993, "Contribution of road passenger transport to meeting greenhouse gas targets: some policy options", *22nd Conference of Economists*, Economic Society of Australia, Murdoch University and Curtin University, Perth, ABARE Conference paper 93(31): 1.

Neil, C & Fopp, R 1992, *Homelessness in Australia: Causes and Consequences*, CSIRO.

Neilson & Associates 1990, Net community benefits of urban consolidation: a case study of Melbourne Australia, Paper presented to the Globe '90 Conference, Vancouver, March.

Neilson, L & Spiller, M 1992, Managing the cities for national economic development, Paper presented to the Biennial Congress of the Royal Australian Planning Institute, Local Government Planners Associations, and Australian Association of Consulting Planners, *Planning for Sustainable Development – Solutions for the 90s*, Canberra, 26-30 April.

Neutze, M 1975, "Urban land policy in five western countries", *Journal of Social Policy*, 4: 225.

—— 1982, "Urban planning, policy and management", *Australian Journal of Public Administration*, 41(2): 145.

—— 1994, The costs of urban physical infrastructure services, Urban Research Program, Working paper 42, Research School of Social Sciences, Australian National University, Canberra.

Neutze, M & Kendig, H 1991, "Achievement of home ownership among post-war Australian cohorts", *Housing Studies*, 6(1): 3.

Newman, PWG 1982, "Domestic energy use in Australian Cities", *Urban Ecology*, 7.

Organisation for Economic Co-operationa and Development (OECD) 1990, Environmental Policies for Cities in the 1990s, OECD, Paris.

Orski, CK 1990, "Can management & transportation help solve our growing traffic congestion and air pollution problems?", *Transportation Quarterly*, 44(4): 483.

Our Common Future 1991, ESD newsbrief, Issue No 2, July.

Pearce, D, Barbier, E & Markandya, A 1990, *Sustainable Development, Economics and Environment in the Third World*, Edward Elgar.

Pearce, D, Markandya, A & Barbier, E 1989, *Blueprint for a Green Economy*, Earthscan Publications Ltd.

Peel, M 1995, The redevelopment of public housing estates: before and after, Seminar presented at the Urban Research Program seminar series, Research School of Social Sciences, Australian National University, May.

Prime Minister's Urban Design Taskforce 1994, *Urban Design in Australia*, Report [Mant report], AGPS.

Reiger, K 1985, *The Disenchantment of the Home: Modernising Australian Democratic Life*, Oxford University Press.

Reiger, K 1991, *Family Economy*, McPhee Gribble.

Rodger, A & Fay, R 1991, "Sustainable suburbia", *Exedra* , 3(1): 4.

Rosenberg , NJ, Easterling, WE, III, Crossnon, PR & Darmstadter, J 1989, *Greenhouse Warming: Abatement and Adaptation, Resources for the Future*, Washington DC.

Runnalls, D 1991, "Environmental management or management for sustainable development?", (Keynote address) in *Environmental Management in Developing Countries*, OECD.

Rybczynski, W 1986, *Home: The Short History of an Idea*, Penguin Books.

Sandercock, L 1975, *Cities for Sale: Property, Politics and Planning in Australia*, Melbourne University Press.

Schramm, G & Warford, JJ (eds) 1989, *Environmental Management and Economic Development*, Johns Hopkins University Press.

Scitovsky, T 1976, *The Joyless Economy: An Inquiry into Human Satisfaction and Consumer Dissatisfaction*, Oxford University Press.

—— 1986, *Human Desire and Economic Satisfaction: Essays on the Frontiers of Economics*, New York University Press.

Scott Carver Pty Ltd 1992, *Review of Medium/High Density Residential Controls*, Department of Planning, Urban Consolidation and Design, Sydney.

Self, P 1993, *Government by the Market: The Politics of Public Choice*, Macmillan.

Sharpe, R 1978, "The effect of urban form on transport energy patterns", *Urban Ecology*, 3: 125.

Sharpe, R 1982, "Energy efficiency and equity of various urban land use patterns", *Urban Ecology*, 7.

Simon, D 1989, "Sustainable development: theoretical construct or attainable goal?", *Environmental Conservation*, 16 (1) Spring.

Sorte, G (nd) Perception of public green space—a park for homo urbaniensis, Department of Landscape Planning, Swedish University of Agricultural Sciences, Alnarp [mimeo].

Spiller, M 1992, Federal initiatives on better cities, Paper presented to the Winter Planning Seminar of the Planning Education Foundation of South Australia, The Royal Australian Planning Institute (SA Division); The South Australian Local Government Planners Association; and National Environmental Law Association (SA Division) , Adelaide, 29-30 July.

Starke, L 1990, *Signs of Hope: Working Towards our Common Future*, Oxford University Press.

Stevens, C, Baum, S & Hassan, R 1992, "The housing and location preferences of Adelaide residents", *Urban Policy and Research*, 10(3): 6.

Stevenson, A, Martin, E & O'Neill, J 1967, *High Living: A Study of Family Life in Flats*, Melbourne University Press.

Stilwell, F 1986, *The Accord and Beyond: The Political Economy of the Labor Government*, Pluto Press.

—— 1992, *Understanding Cities and Regions*, Pluto Press.

—— 1993, *Reshaping Australia: Urban Problems and Policies*, Pluto Press.

—— 1994a, *Australian Urban and Regional Development: The Policy Challenge*, Parliamentary Research Service, Department of the Parliamentary Library.

—— 1994b, "Working nation: from green to white paper", *Journal of Australian Political Economy*, 33, June.

Stretton, H 1970, *Ideas for Australian Cities*, Georgian House.

—— 1974, *Housing and Government*, The Boyer Lectures, ABC, Sydney.

—— 1987, "Housing policies past and future", in *Political Essays*, Georgian House.

—— 1988, "Housing—an investment for all", in *Urban Planning in Australia: Critical Readings*, (eds) JB McLoughlin & M Huxley, Longman.

Submission by Planning Review to the Industry Commission Inquiry into Taxation and Financial Policy Impacts on Urban Settlement, *The Role of the State Government in the Provision of Urban Infrastructure, Pricing and Financing of Urban Infrastructure, Infrastructure Financing*, April 1992 [submission No 56].

Submission by the Australian Capital Territory Government to the Industry Commission Inquiry into Taxation and Financial Policy Impacts on Urban Settlement, *Planning to Keep Canberra Canberra: Labor's Land and Planning Policy*, May 1992 [submission No 71].

—— *The Urban Development of Canberra*, April 1992 [submission No 63].

Submission by the City of Melbourne to the Industry Commission Inquiry into Taxation and Financial Policy Impacts on Urban Settlement, March 1992 [submission No 25].

—— March 1992 [submission No 75].

Submission by the Hunter Water Corporation to the Industry Commission Inquiry into Taxation and Financial Policy Impacts on Urban Settlement, April 1992 [submission No 55].

Submission by the South Australia Planning Review to the Industry Commission Inquiry into Taxation and Financial Policy Impacts on Urban Settlement, July 1992 [submission No 87].

Submission by the Water Authority of Western Australia to the Industry Commission Inquiry into Taxation and Financial Policy Impacts on Urban Settlement, May 1992 [submission No 58]

Submission from the Department of Health, Housing and Community Services to the Industry Commission Inquiry into Taxation and Financial Policy Impacts on Urban Settlement, June 1992, [no submission number].

Sydney Regional Environment Plan No 1, 1980, Department of Environment and Planning, Sydney, December.

Sydney Regional Environment Plan No 2, 1981, Department of Environment and Planning, Sydney, December.

Sydney Regional Environment Plan No 12, 1987, Department of Planning, Sydney.

Thorne, R 1991, "Housing as 'home' in the Australian context", *People and Physical Environment Research,* 36: 54.

Travers Morgan Pty Ltd & Applied Economics Pty Ltd 1991a, *Housing Costs Study, no 1, Costs of New Housing Developments,* DITAC & DHHCS.

—— 1991b, *Housing Costs Study, no 2, Evaluation of Fringe Development and Urban Consolidation,* DITAC & DHHCS.

—— 1991c, *Housing Costs Study, no 3, Determinants of the Prices of Established Housing,* DITAC & DHHCS.

Treloar, G 1993, "Embodied energy analysis of buildings—part 2: a case study", *Exedra,* 4(1): 11.

Troy, P 1971, Environmental Quality in Four Sydney Suburban Areas, Urban Research Unit monograph, Research School of Social Sciences, Australian National University.

—— 1972, Environmental Quality in Four Melbourne Suburban Areas, Urban Research Unit monograph, Research School of Social Sciences, Australian National University.

—— 1988, "Government housing policy in New South Wales 1788–1900", *Housing Studies,* 3(1): 20.

—— 1990, "The greenhouse effect and the city", *Australian Planner,* 28(1): 17.

—— 1991, The benefits of owner occupation, Urban Research Program, Working paper 39, Research School of Social Sciences, Australian National University.

—— 1992a, "Defending the quarter-acre block against the new feudalism, *Town and Country Planning,* 61(9): 240.

—— 1992b, "The new feudalsim", *Urban Futures,* 2(2): 36.

Tucker, SN & Treloar, GJ 1994, "Energy embodied in construction and refurbishment of buildings", in *Buildings and Environment, Proceedings of the first International Conference,* Building Research Establishment, Watford, UK.

Tucker, SN, Salomonsson, GD & Macsporran, C 1994, "Energy implications of building materials recycling", in *Buildings and the Environment, Proceedings of the First International Conference,* Building Research Establishment, Watford, UK.

VICCODE, Victorian State Planning Code,

VICCODE, 2 1994, Review reported in December.

Victorian Energy Planning Program 1985, *Victoria's Energy: Strategy & Policy Options,* Department of Industry, Technology & Resources, Victoria.

Victorian Strategic Transport Study (VSTS) 1992, *Monitoring Victoria's Transport,* Report prepared by the Department of Geography & Environmental Science, Monash University and the Transport Research Centre, University of Melbourne [this document the first in a periodic series to monitor the Victoria transport system and industry].

Walker, IJ & Lyall, KD 1989, "The potential for reduced CO_2 emissions through increased energy efficiency and the use of renewable energy technologies in Australia", in *Energy Technologies for Reducing Emissions of Greenhouse Gases: Proceedings of an Expert's Seminar*, OECD, Paris.

Walsh, P 1988, Address by the Minister for Finance, Senator Peter Walsh, to a Conference organised by Price Waterhouse, Urwick Sydney, Friday 17 June.

Winston, D 1957, *Sydney's Great Experiment: the Progress of the Cumberland County Plan*, Angus & Robertson.

Woodhead, WD 1991, *A Study into the Economics of Medium Density Housing*, Report prepared for the Office of Housing, Department of Housing and Construction, South Australia, CSIRO Division of Building, Construction and Engineering, April.

—— 1994, "The economics of higher density housing", *Urban Futures*, 3(4) and 4(1): 43.

World Commission on Environment and Development 1987, *Our Common Future*, Oxford University Press.

INDEX

INDEX